# GCS
# Revision
## RESCUE



# PHYSICS
## FOR DOUBLE SCIENCE

Jim Breithaupt

Hodder & Stoughton
A MEMBER OF THE HODDER HEADLINE GROUP

A catalogue record for this title is available from the British Library.

ISBN 0340 775 661

First published 2000
Impression number 10 9 8 7 6 5 4 3 2 1
Year 2005 2004 2003 2002 2001 2000



Editorial, design and production by Hart McLeod, Cambridge

Printed in Spain by Graphycems for Hodder & Stoughton Educational, a division of Hodder Headline Plc
338 Euston Road, London NW1 3BH

# Contents

# Revision Rescue

The pages that follow contain a gold mine of information on how you can achieve success in your exams. Read them and apply the information, and you will be able to spend less, but more efficient, time studying, with better results.

This section gives you vital information on how to remember more while you are learning and how to remember more after you have finished studying. It explains

- how to use special techniques to improve your memory
- how to use a revolutionary note-taking technique called Mind Mapping that will double your memory and help you to write essays and answer exam questions
- how to read everything faster while at the same time improving your comprehension and concentration

## Your amazing memory

There are five important things you must know about your brain and memory to revolutionise your school life.

1 how your memory ('recall') works while you are learning

2 how your memory works after you have finished learning

3 how to use Mind Maps – a special technique for helping you with all aspects of your studies

4 how to increase your reading speed

5 how to zap your revision

## 1 Recall during learning – the need for breaks

When you are studying, your memory can concentrate, understand and remember well for between 20 and 45 minutes at a time. Then it needs a break. If you carry on for longer than this without one, your memory starts to break down! If you study for hours non-stop, you will remember only a fraction of what you have been trying to learn, and you will have wasted valuable revision time.

So, ideally, study for less than an hour, then take a five- to ten-minute break. During the break listen to music, go for a walk, do some exercise, or just daydream. (Daydreaming is a necessary brain-power booster – geniuses do it regularly.) During the break your brain will be sorting out what it has been learning, and you will go back to your books with the new information safely stored and organised in your memory banks.

## 2 Recall after learning – the waves of your memory

What do you think begins to happen to your memory straight after you have finished learning something? Does it immediately start forgetting? No! Your brain actually increases its power and carries on remembering. For a short time after your study session, your brain integrates the information, making a more complete picture of everything it has just learnt. Only then does the rapid decline in memory begin, and as much as 80 per cent of what you have learnt can be forgotten in a day.

However, if you catch the top of the wave of your memory, and briefly review (look back over) what you have been revising at the correct time, the memory is stamped in far more strongly, and stays at the crest of the wave for a much longer time. To maximise your brain's power to remember, take a few minutes and use a Mind Map to review what you have learnt at the end of a day. Then review it at the end of a week, again at the end of the month, and finally a week before the exams. That way you'll ride your memory wave all the way to your exam – and beyond!

Amazing as your memory is (think of everything you actually have stored in your brain at this moment) the principles on which it operates are very simple. Your brain will remember if it:

(a) has an image (a picture or a symbol);

(b) has that image fixed

(c) can link that image to something else.

## 3 The Mind Map® – a picture of the way you think

Do you like taking notes? More importantly, do you like having to go back over and learn them before exams? Most students I know certainly do not! And how do you take your notes? Most people take notes on lined paper, using blue or black ink. The result, visually, is boring! And what does your brain do when it is bored? It turns off, tunes out, and goes to sleep! Add a dash of colour, rhythm, imagination, and the whole note-taking process becomes much more fun, uses more of your brain's abilities, and improves your recall and understanding.

A Mind Map mirrors the way your brain works. It can be used for note-taking from books or in class, for reviewing what you have just studied, for revising, and for essay planning for coursework and in exams. It uses all your memory's natural techniques to build up your rapidly growing 'memory muscle'.

You will find sample Mind Maps at the end of this book. Study them, add some colour, personalise them, and then have a go at drawing your own – you'll remember them far better! Put them on your walls and in your files for a quick-and-easy review of the topic.

## How to draw a Mind Map®

1 Start in the middle of the page with the page turned sideways. This gives your brain the maximum room for its thoughts.

2 Always start by drawing a small picture or symbol. Why? Because a picture is worth a thousand words to your brain. And try to use at least three colours, as colour helps your memory even more.

3 Let your thoughts flow, and write or draw your ideas on coloured branching lines connected to your central image. These key symbols and words are the headings for your topic.

4 Then add facts and ideas by drawing more, smaller, branches on to the appropriate main branches, just like a tree.

5 Always print your word clearly on its line. Use only one word per line.

6 To link ideas and on different branches, use arrows, colours, underlining and boxes.

## How to read a Mind Map®

1 Begin in the centre, the focus of your topic.

2 The words/images attached to the centre are like chapter headings, so read them next.

3 Always read out from the centre, in every direction (even on the left-hand side, where you will have to read from right to left, instead of the usual left to right).

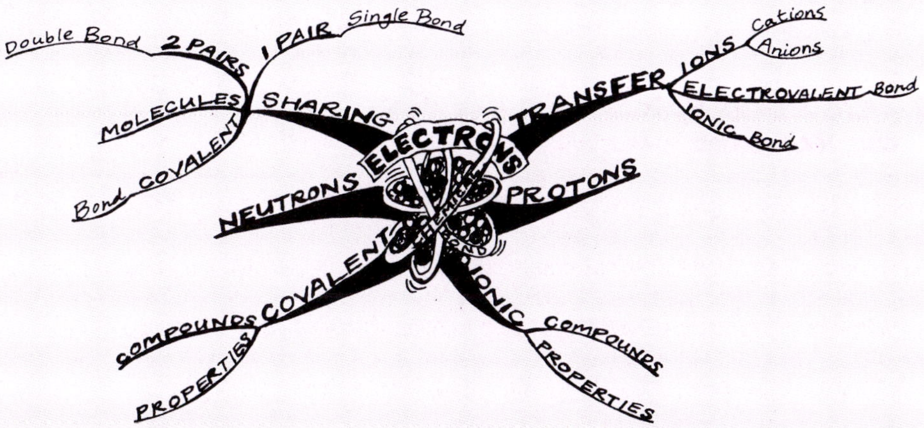

## 4 Super speed reading

It seems incredible, but it's been proved – the faster you read, the more you understand and remember! So here are some tips to help you to practise reading faster – you'll cover the ground more quickly, remember more, and have more time for revision!

First read the whole text (whether it's a lengthy book or an exam paper) very quickly, to give your brain an overall idea of what's ahead and get it working. (It's like sending out a scout to look at the territory you have to cover – it's much easier when you know what to expect!) Then read the text again for more detailed information.

Have the text a reasonable distance away from your eyes. In this way your eye/brain system will be able to see more at a glance, and will naturally begin to read faster.

Take in groups of words at a time. Rather than reading 'slowly and carefully' read faster, more enthusiastically. Your comprehension will rocket!

Take in phrases rather than single words while you read.

Use a guide. Your eyes are designed to follow movement, so a thin pencil underneath the lines you are reading, moved smoothly along, will 'pull' your eyes to faster speeds.

## 5 And finally...

Have fun while you learn – studies show that those people who enjoy what they are doing understand and remember it more, and generally do it better.

Use your teachers as resource centres. Ask them for help with specific topics and with more general advice on how you can improve your all-round performance.

Personalise your Revision Rescue by underlining and highlighting, by adding notes and pictures. Allow your brain to have a conversation with it!

**Tony Buzan**

## How to use this book

*Revision Rescue: Physics for Double Science* is clearly divided into subject chapters and topic sections. Each contains the facts you need to know, with key words highlighted for extra clarity.

The tinted boxes contain useful tips and hints, words and ideas to remember and short quizzes to test your knowledge and highlight areas that you may need to revise again.

Each chapter ends with a longer quiz related to the topic covered.

## The Exam Emergency Service on Teletext

Teletext

As you revise, you can boost your knowledge even further with a free exam emergency service on Teletext.

At key revision times, this service offers subject-specific advice, tips and hints for effective exam performance and guidance for planning you revision... until the very last minute! You will find a wide range of subject quizzes, which change regularly so you can test your knowledge again and again.

# The Earth in space 1

## About the Earth

- The Earth **spins** steadily about its poles, taking **24 hours** for a full turn.
- The **sunlit** half of the Earth faces towards the Sun, the **dark** half faces away from the Sun.
- Every point on the Earth is in daylight as it passes through the sunlit side of the Earth, and in darkness passing through the night side of the Earth.
- **Sunrise** is when we move from darkness to daylight.
- **Sunset** is when we move from daylight to darkness.
- The **stars** cannot be seen in daylight because the Sun makes the sky too bright. At night, we can see the stars because they are in the opposite direction from the Sun.
- The Earth moves on an almost circular **orbit** round the Sun and takes 365¼ days to go round the Sun once.
- The **Earth's axis is tilted** towards the Pole Star; in the northern hemisphere in summer the north pole is tilted towards the Sun and in winter the north pole is tilted away from the Sun.
- The Sun rises on the **eastern** horizon and sets on the **western** horizon. At mid-day, the Sun is due **south**.

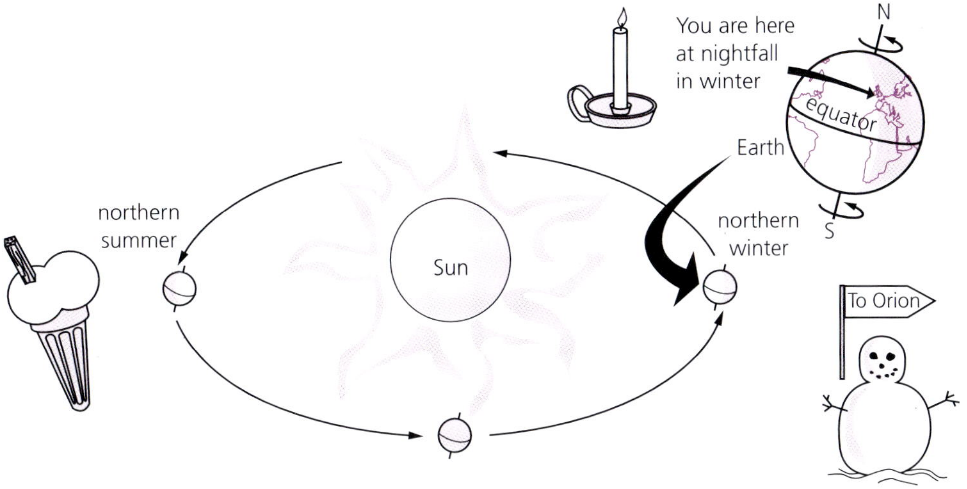

# Phases and eclipses

## The phases of the Moon

These are due to how much of the Moon's sunlit face can be seen from the Earth.

- At full Moon, the Moon lies in the opposite direction from the Sun.
- At new Moon, the Moon lies between the Sun and the Earth.
- At half Moon, the Moon lies at 90° to the line between the Sun and the Earth.
- One complete cycle of phases takes just over 28 days.

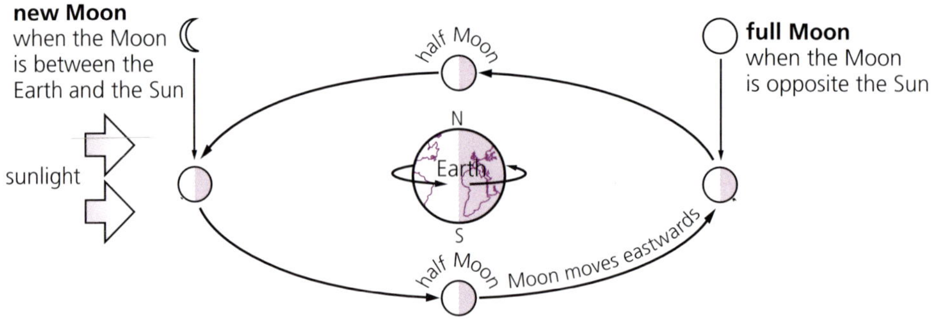


### Complete the word puzzle

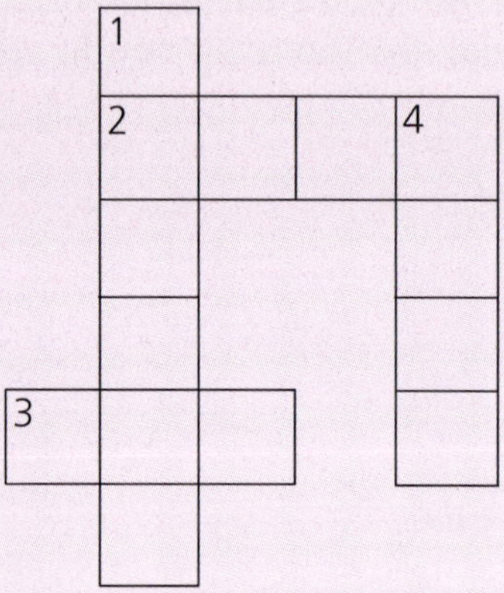


1. The name for the Moon's changing appearance in the sky.
2. We see this fraction of the Moon's sunlit surface when the Moon is at 90° to the line from the Sun to the Earth.
3. A _______?_______ moon is seen when the Moon is between the Sun and the Earth.
4. A _______?_______ moon is seen about 14 days after 3.

**Answers**
1. (phases)
2. (half)
3. (new)
4. (full)

## Eclipses

When an eclipse happens, the Moon is on the line between the centre of the Sun and the Earth's centre. Eclipses do not occur every month because the Moon's orbit is tilted to the Earth's orbit.

A **solar eclipse** happens when the Earth passes through the Moon's shadow. During a solar eclipse, the Moon is in the same direction from the Earth as the Sun. A total solar eclipse covers only a small fraction of the Earth's surface.

A solar eclipse is a day-time event, only visible from the day-time half of the Earth.

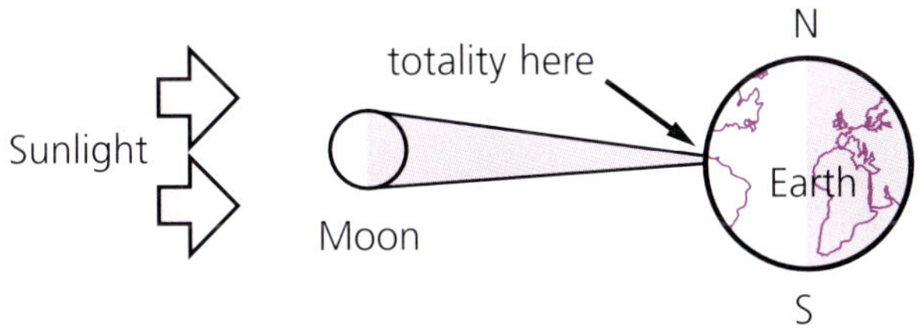


**solar eclipse** when the Moon passes between the Sun and the Earth

A **lunar eclipse** happens when the Moon passes through the Earth's shadow. During a lunar eclipse, the Moon is exactly in the opposite direction to the Sun. Everyone on the night-time half of the Earth can see the eclipse if the sky is clear.

A lunar eclipse can only be seen from the night-time half of the Earth.

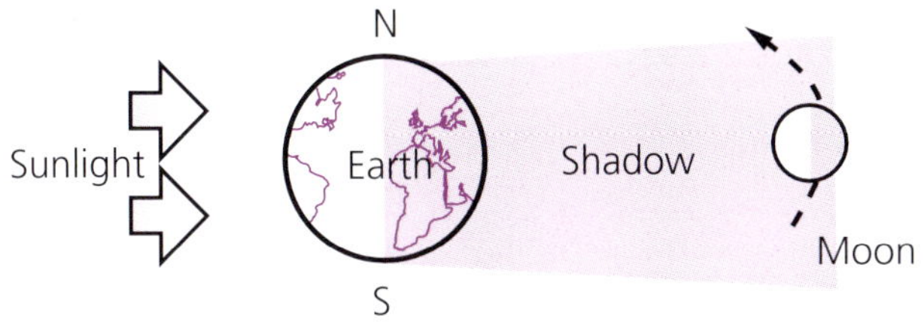


**lunar eclipse** when the Earth passes between the Sun and the Moon

# The planets

The **Solar System** consists of the Sun, the planets and their moons, the minor planets, asteroids and comets. The planets in order of increasing distance from the Sun are:

**M**ercury **V**enus **E**arth **M**ars **J**upiter **S**aturn **U**ranus **N**eptune **P**luto.

*Hint to help you remember:*

***M**ake **V**ery **E**asy **M**ash **J**ust **S**tart **U**sing **N**ew **P**otatoes.*

- We can see the other planets because they reflect sunlight; the brightness of a planet depends on its distance from Earth and its position relative to the Earth and the Sun.
- The planets move round the Sun in the same direction and in almost the same plane; the orbit of each planet is almost circular, except for Pluto which is sometimes closer than Neptune to the Sun.
- Mercury, Venus, Earth, Mars and Pluto are rocky planets.
- Jupiter, Saturn, Uranus and Neptune are giant gas planets.
- Mercury has no atmosphere.
- The surface of Venus is permanently covered by clouds.
- Mars is the most Earth-like planet.
- Jupiter is the largest planet.
- Saturn has a ring system; the orientation of its rings affects its brightness.
- Neptune, Uranus and Pluto can only be seen with a telescope.

## Quick quiz

1. Name the 5 rocky planets.
2. Name the 4 giant gas planets.
3. What does Saturn have that no other planet seen from Earth has?
4. What doesn't Mercury have that Venus, Earth and Mars have?
5. Name the planets in order of distance from the Sun.

**Answers**

1. Mercury Venus Earth Mars Pluto
2. Jupiter Saturn Uranus Neptune
3. rings
4. an atmosphere
5. Mercury Venus Earth Mars Jupiter Saturn Uranus Neptune Pluto

# Planetary distances

The distance to another planet from Earth changes as the planet moves round its orbit relative to the Earth.

## The inner planets

Mercury and Venus are closer to the Sun than the Earth.

- When an inner planet is **nearest to Earth**, it lies between the Sun and the Earth.
- When an inner planet is **furthest from Earth**, it lies on the other side of the Sun to the Earth.

## The outer planets

All the other planets apart from Mercury and Venus orbit the Sun beyond the Earth.

- When an outer planet is **nearest to Earth**, it lies in the opposite direction to the Sun.
- When an outer planet is **furthest from Earth**, it lies on the other side of the Sun.

## Maximum and minimum distances to the planets

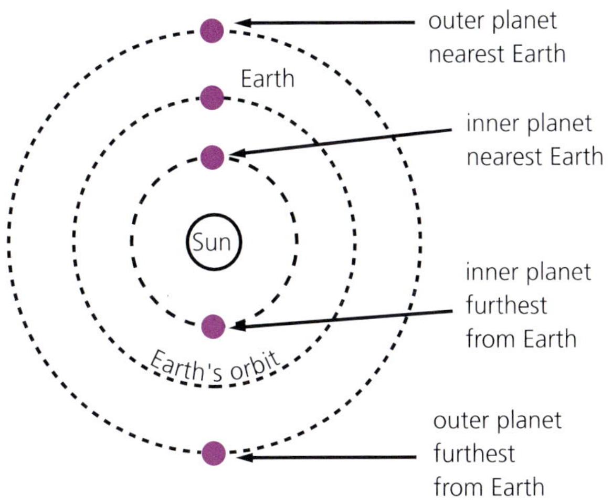

# Gravity

- Gravity is an attractive **force** that acts between any two objects; the force of gravity is **greater** the greater the **masses** of the two objects, and the **nearer** the two objects are.
- The force of gravity due to the Earth on an object of mass 1 kg at the Earth's surface is 10 N.
- The force of gravity of the Sun on a planet always acts towards the centre of the Sun; the larger the radius of orbit of a planet, the longer the planet takes to orbit the Sun.

## Satellites

A satellite stays in orbit because of the force of gravity between the satellite and the Earth. The **Moon**, the only natural satellite of the Earth, takes 27¼ days to orbit the Earth. The further a satellite is from the Earth, the longer it takes to go round its orbit. Satellites are used for communications, weather forecasts, security and surveying. Communication satellites are in **geostationary** orbits (i.e. time for each orbit = 24 hours exactly) directly above the Equator.

## In orbit

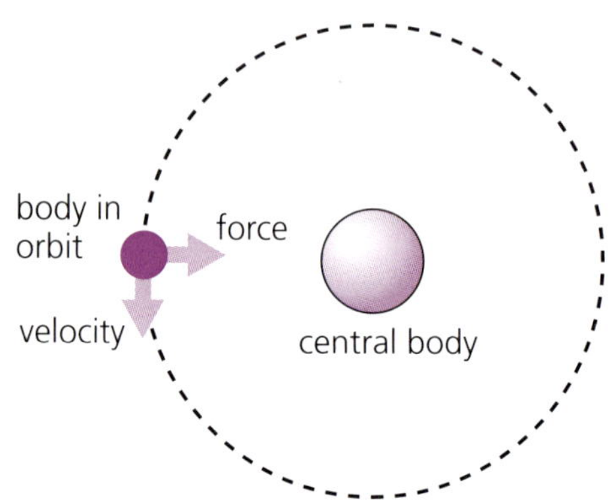


'Geostationary' means stationary relative to the Earth, so a geostationary satellite is always above the same point on the Equator.

# Comets

- A comet moves round the Sun on an **elliptical** orbit, usually in a different plane from the planets.
- The **speed** of a comet is greater the nearer it is to the Sun. The longer a comet takes for each orbit, the further from the Sun it goes.
- The **time** taken by a comet to move once round its orbit is the same for every orbit.
- A comet **glows** due to solar heating when it is near the Sun and is **dark** and invisible when far from the Sun.
- A comet's **tail** of glowing gas and dust is due to the **solar wind** and always points away from the Sun.

## A comet orbit

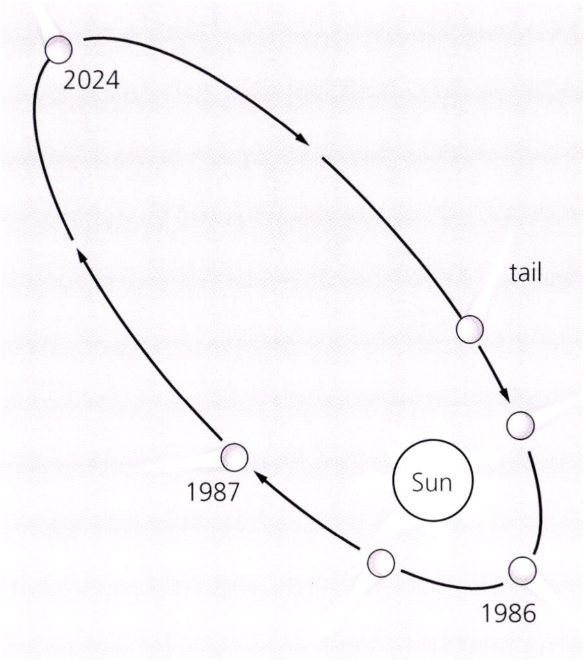

# The life-cycle of a star

**Stars** are giant balls of glowing gas that emit electromagnetic radiation and high-energy particles. The brightness of a star depends on how much power it emits and how far away it is.

**The Sun**, the nearest star to the Earth, will swell up to become a red giant when it has fused all its hydrogen nuclei into helium nuclei. A **red giant** star releases energy due to fusion of helium nuclei into heavier nuclei. When no more helium is available the star will collapse to become a **white dwarf**. A **supernova** is an exploding star. This happens to stars which are much more massive than the Sun because they collapse into unstable white dwarfs.

## The life-cycle of a star

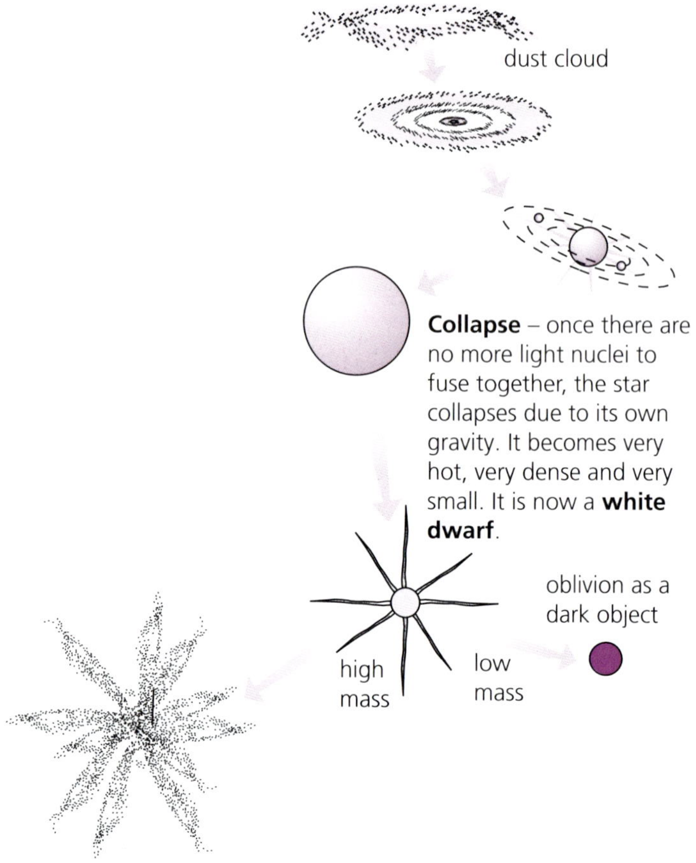


**Explosion** – if the star is massive enough, it will explode, releasing huge amounts of matter and radiation in a very short time. This **supernova** event is thought to leave behind an extremely dense object known as a **neutron** star.

# Galaxies

- A galaxy contains billions of stars, held together by gravity.
- The Sun is one of billions of stars in a spiral galaxy called the **Milky Way**.
- We see the Milky Way from the inside.
- Light takes about 100,000 years to cross the Milky Way galaxy.
- The stars we can see in the night sky are also in the Milky Way.
- The **Universe** contains a huge number of galaxies which are separated by empty space.
- Light takes about a million years to reach us from the nearest galaxy and about 10,000 million years from the furthest galaxy.
- Light from distant galaxies is **red-shifted** towards longer wavelengths. This happens because these galaxies are **receding** (i.e. moving away) from us at speeds approaching the speed of light.

## Starlight spectra

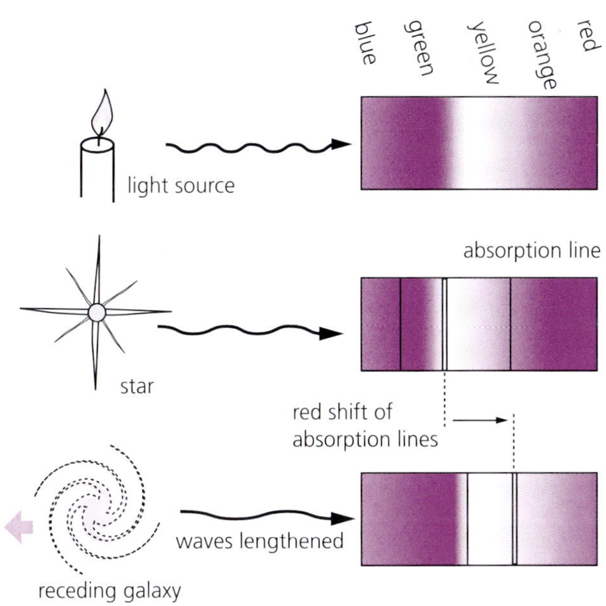

# The expanding Universe and the Big Bang

## Hubble's law

The speed of recession of a distant galaxy can be worked out from its starlight red-shift. Hubble measured the red-shift (i.e. increase of wavelength) for a large number of galaxies at known distances. He then worked out the speed of each galaxy. He discovered that the speed is proportional to the distance from Earth. The more distant a galaxy is, the faster it is moving away from us.

**Hubble's law states that:**

- the galaxies are receding (moving away) from us
- the speed of recession of a galaxy is proportional to its distance from us.

## The Big Bang

All the distant galaxies are moving away from us and from each other. This is because the Universe is expanding. This expansion is thought to have originated from a massive explosion we refer to as the Big Bang.
This is thought to have taken place between 10,000 and 15,000 million years ago.

**Evidence for the Big Bang:**

- Hubble's law
- radiation from the Big Bang has been detected as microwaves coming from all directions (microwave radiation is electromagnetic radiation in the wavelength range from about 0.1 mm to about 100 mm)
- a correct prediction of the proportion of hydrogen to helium in the Universe.

### Remember

'Receding' means moving away.

'Red-shift' of light means an increase of its wavelength.

# The Earth in space quiz

## Questions

1 Which direction is the Sun at mid-day?

2 Why does the Sun rise every 24 hours?

3 (a) At full Moon, where is the Moon in relation to the Sun and the Earth?
(b) During a solar eclipse, where is the Moon in relation to the Sun and the Earth?

4 (a) Which is the largest planet? (b) Which planet is most like the Earth?

5 Why is it never possible to see Venus at midnight?

6 Why does the tail of a comet always point away from the Sun?

7 Why does a comet speed up as it approaches the Sun?

8 What is a white dwarf?

9 What is meant by the term 'red-shift'?

10 State Hubble's law.

**Answers**

**1** South **2** We experience sunrise once every 24 hours when we move from the dark half of the Earth to the sunlit half **3** (a) In the opposite direction from the Sun (b) In the same direction as the Sun **4** (a) Jupiter (b) Mars **5** As seen from Earth, Venus can never be in the opposite direction from the Sun as it is closer than the Earth to the Sun **6** The solar wind consisting of particles and radiation from the Sun causes it to point away from the Sun **7** The force of gravity on it due to the Sun increases as its distance from the Sun decreases **8** A collapsed star **9** The increase of wavelength of light from a star or galaxy due to its motion away from us **10** The speed of recession of a distant galaxy is proportional to its distance from us

# Waves 2

## Types of waves

All waves except electromagnetic waves are carried by a substance. When the particles in one part of a substance are forced to vibrate, the vibrations spread out to other parts of the substance in waves. Electromagnetic waves consist of vibrating electric and magnetic fields linked together without any substance necessary.

### Longitudinal waves

The vibrations of a substance are parallel to the direction of propagation (i.e. travel) of the wave (e.g. primary seismic waves, sound waves, ultrasonics).

### Transverse waves

The vibrations of a substance are at right angles to the direction of propagation of the wave (e.g. waves on a string or a rope, secondary seismic waves, all electromagnetic waves).

Transverse waves are said to be **polarised** if the vibrations are in one plane only. If the vibrations change from one plane to another, the waves are said to be **unpolarised**. Unpolarised waves can be polarised by directing the waves at a filter that only passes waves through that vibrate in one plane only. Light from a filament bulb is unpolarised and can be polarised by passing it through a polaroid filter.

*A plane is a flat area, e.g. the surface of a snooker table is usually in a horizontal plane!*

### Quick quiz

State whether each type of wave in the list below is longitudinal or transverse.

electromagnetic waves, primary seismic waves, secondary seismic waves, sound waves, ultrasonics, waves on a string

**Answers**

Longitudinal:
primary seismic waves
sound waves
ultrasonics
Transverse:
electromagnetic waves
secondary seismic waves
waves on a string

# Wave measurements

- One complete **cycle of vibration** takes a vibrating particle back to the same position and direction as it had at the start of the cycle.
- The **amplitude** is the height of the wave crest above the centre.
- The **wavelength** is the distance from one wave to the next.
- The **frequency** is the number of crests per second passing a point.
- **Wave equation**

  speed = frequency x wavelength.
  (in m/s) (in Hz) (in m)

- Rearranging the equation gives

$$\text{frequency} = \frac{\text{speed}}{\text{wavelength}} \quad \text{or}$$

$$\text{wavelength} = \frac{\text{speed}}{\text{frequency}}.$$

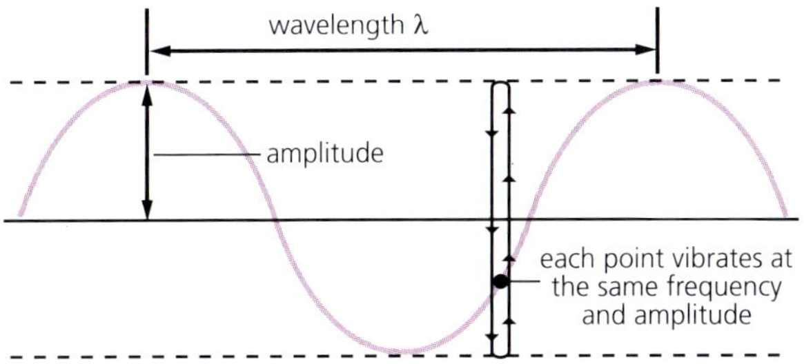


## Quick quiz

Use the following word list to fill in the spaces below.

amplitude frequency hertz wavelength

1. The number of wave crests passing a point in one second is the ________________.
2. The __________ is the height of a wave from the middle.
3. Speed = frequency x ________________.
4. The unit of frequency is the________________.

**Answers**

1. frequency
2. amplitude
3. wavelength
4. hertz

# Wave properties

## Reflection

The angle of reflection of a plane wave to a straight boundary = the angle of incidence.

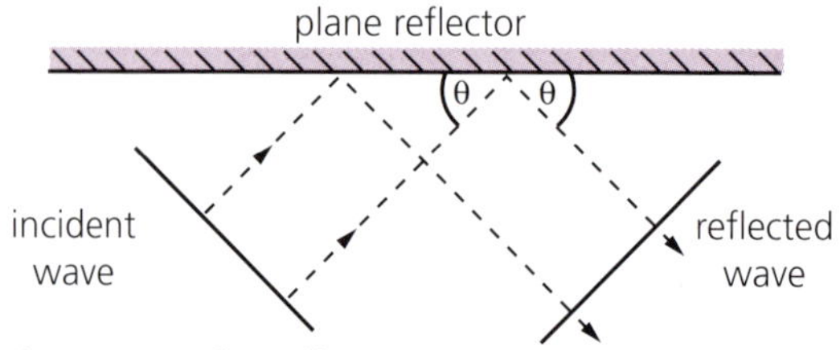


Plane waves reflect off a straight reflector at the same angle to its surface as they hit it. The reflected waves are at the same angle to the normal as the incident waves.

## Refraction

Waves that pass through a boundary at an angle to the boundary change direction.

## Diffraction

Waves that pass through a gap or round an obstacle spread out after the gap or obstacle. The narrower the gap or the longer the wavelength, the greater the spreading.

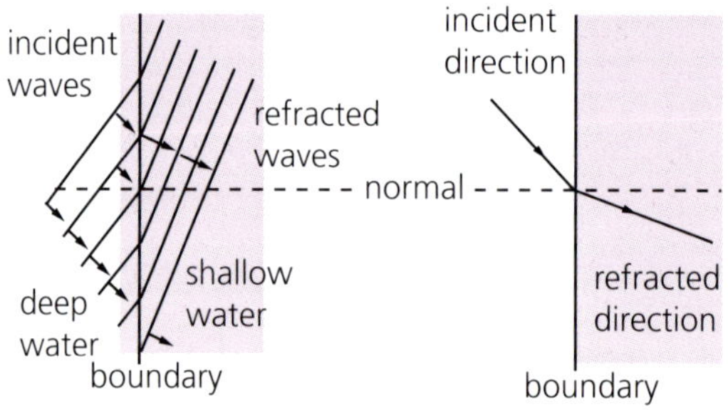

# Sound waves

## The nature of sound

- Sound waves are vibrations of the particles of a substance.
- Sound waves are longitudinal.
- Sound frequencies up to about 18 kHz can be detected by a normal ear.
- Sound cannot travel through a vacuum.
- The **loudness** of a sound is increased by increasing the **amplitude** of the sound wave.
- The loudness level of a sound is measured in **decibels**.
- The **pitch** of a sound is increased by raising its **frequency**.

## Properties of sound

- **Absorption** – soft surfaces absorb sound better than hard surfaces.
- **Reflection** – a hard surface reflects sound.
- **Refraction** – sound waves in air can change direction where the air temperature changes with position because the speed of sound increases with temperature.
- **Diffraction** – sound waves spread out when they pass through a gap.

## Ultrasonics

- **Ultrasound** is sound at frequencies above the upper limit of the human ear (about 18 kHz).
- **Uses** – ultrasonic cleaning, ultrasonic medical scanner, depth finding at sea, testing metals for internal cracks.
- Ultrasonic waves are not harmful as they do not create ions when they pass through a substance (unlike X-rays).

**Sound waves** are vibrations that travel through a substance. Sound travels through solids, liquids and gases. Sound does not travel through a vacuum.

The speed of sound in air is about 340 m/s. In a thunderstorm, unless the storm is overhead, the clap of thunder is heard after a thunderflash because sound travels much slower than light.

$$\text{speed} = \text{frequency} \times \text{wavelength}$$

$$\text{frequency} = \frac{\text{speed}}{\text{wavelength}} \quad \text{or}$$

$$\text{wavelength} = \frac{\text{speed}}{\text{frequency}}.$$

Speed is always on top!

# The structure of the Earth

## The layered structure of the Earth

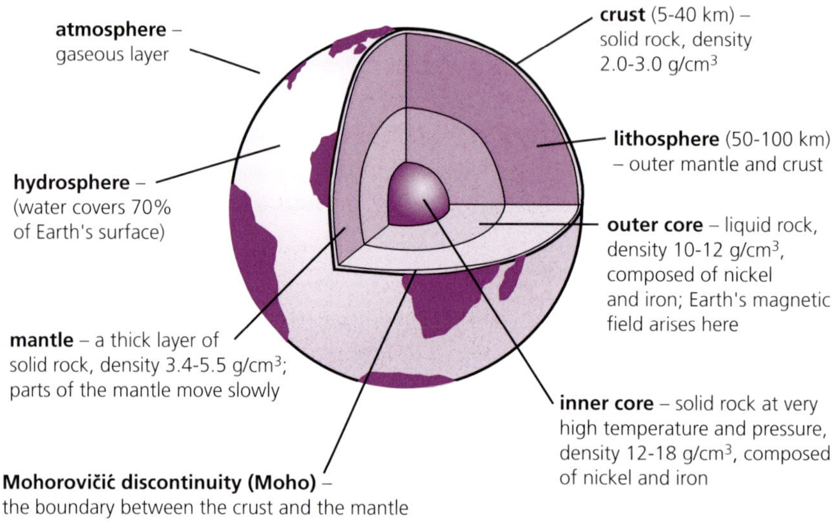


The Earth's crust and outer mantle are made up of **tectonic plates** that carry the continents. The plates are moving very slowly at a rate of about 5 cm per year. The plates push against each other due to their movement, creating stress where they are in contact. An **earthquake** occurs when the energy stored where two plates are in contact is suddenly released.

### Quick quiz

1. Is a) the inner core, b) the crust of the Earth solid or liquid?
2. What is the name for the plates that carry the continents?
3. What causes an earthquake?
4. Name the two regions of the Earth's interior between the inner core and the crust.

**Answers**

1. a) solid, b) solid
2. Tectonic plates
3. Two tectonic plates collide violently.
4. the outer core and the mantle

# Seismic waves

## Seismic waves inside the Earth

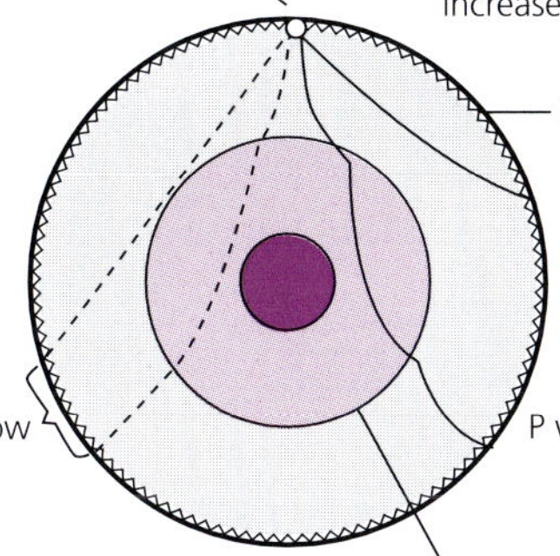


When an earthquake occurs **seismic waves** spread out from the **focus** of the earthquake. The focus is the point where the seismic waves originate from. The **epicentre** of an earthquake is the point on the Earth's surface directly above where the earthquake occurs.

- **Primary** (**P**) waves are longitudinal waves (i.e. push and pull) that arrive first.
- **Secondary** (**S**) waves are transverse waves (i.e. side to side) that arrive after the primary waves.
- **Long** (**L**) waves arrive last because they travel in the crust only, heaving the surface up and down as well as to and fro.
- The **Richter** scale is a 'times ten' scale used to measure the energy released by an earthquake.

### Example

An earthquake at '8' on the Richter scale is 100 times more powerful than one at '6'.

# Reflection of light

## Reflection at a plane mirror

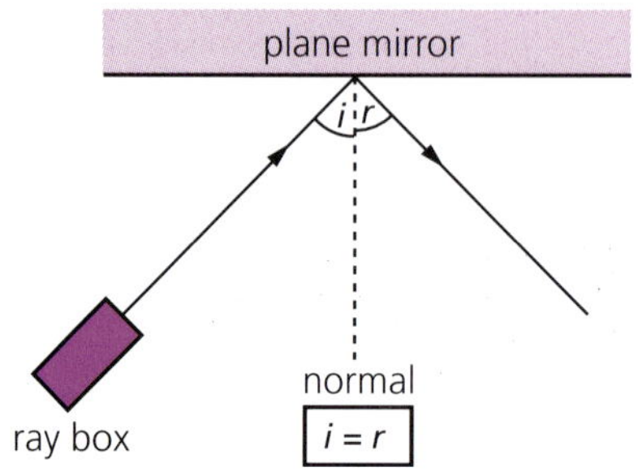


## Image formation in a plane mirror

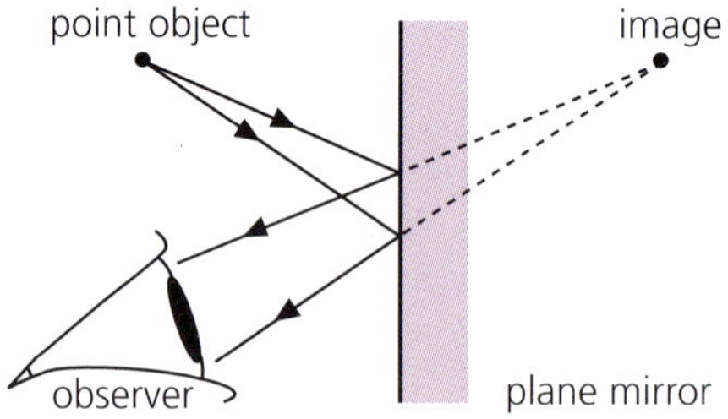


The image of an object in a plane mirror is **virtual** (i.e. formed where the rays appear to come from), the same size as the object, and the same distance from the mirror as the object.

## Uses of mirrors

- **Plane mirror** – wall mirror; periscope; meter scale.
- **Concave mirror** – face mirror; focusing mirror.
- **Convex mirror** – driving mirror; security mirror.

# Refraction of light

Refraction is the change of direction of light when it crosses the boundary between two transparent substances. This is due to a change of speed at the boundary. The greater the change of speed at the boundary between two transparent substances, the greater the change of direction.

## Refraction in a glass block

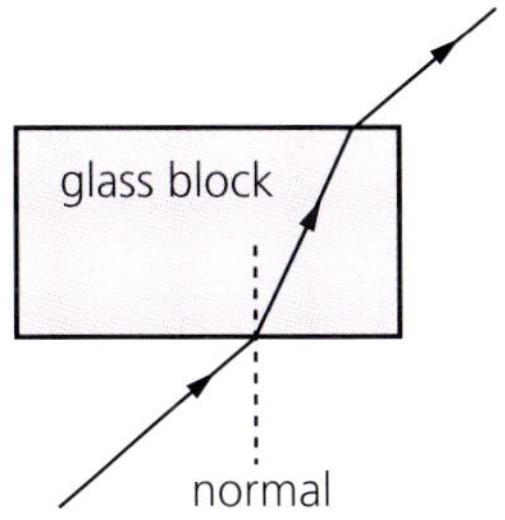


- A light ray refracts towards the normal when it passes from air into a transparent substance (i.e. when its speed is decreased), and away from the normal when it passes from a transparent substance into air (i.e. when its speed is increased).
- The normal is the straight line at right angles to the boundary at the point of incidence. If the incident light ray is along the normal, the light ray continues without change of direction.

- The **refractive index** of a substance

$$= \frac{\text{speed of light in a vacuum}}{\text{speed of light in the substance}}.$$

The greater the refractive index of a substance is, the greater the change of direction when a light ray enters the substance from air.

### Light

- Light travels faster in air than in glass. The speed and the wavelength of light is reduced when it passes into glass from air.
- When a light ray passes from air into glass at a non-zero angle to the normal, it bends towards the normal.
- When a light ray passes from glass into air at a non-zero angle to the normal, it bends away from the normal.

# Total internal reflection

This occurs at the boundary between two transparent substances

- if the refractive index of the incident substance is greater than that of the other substance and
- if the angle of incidence is greater than a certain angle, known as the **critical angle**, which depends on the two substances.

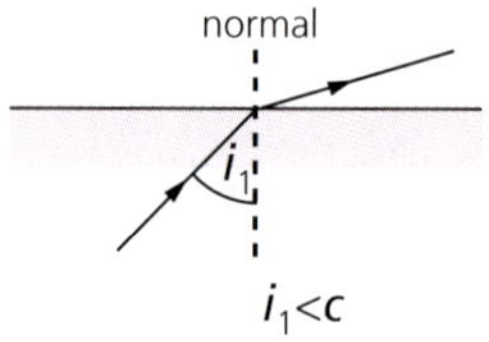


**1** If angle of incidence is less than the critical angle, the light ray bends away from the normal on leaving the glass.

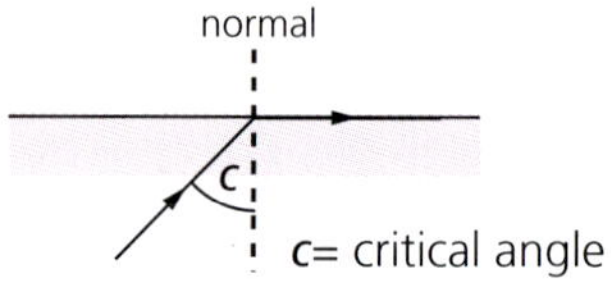


**2** If the angle of incidence is equal to the critical angle, the light refracts along the boundary.

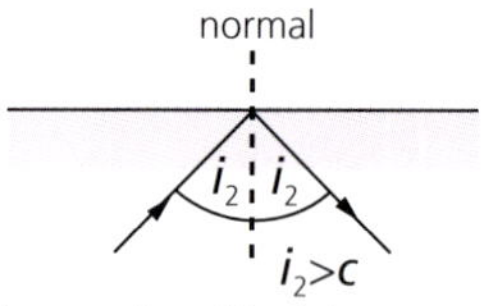


**3** If the angle of incidence exceeds the critical angle, the light ray is totally internally reflected.

**Applications** of total internal reflection include prisms in optical instruments (e.g. binoculars) and optical fibres used in medicine and communications.

## An optical fibre

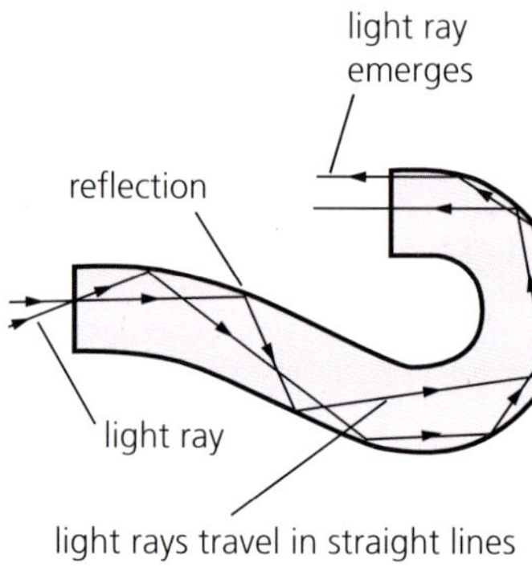

# Lenses

## Focal point of a lens

For a **convex lens** the focal point is where a parallel beam of light along the lens axis is brought to a focus by the lens.

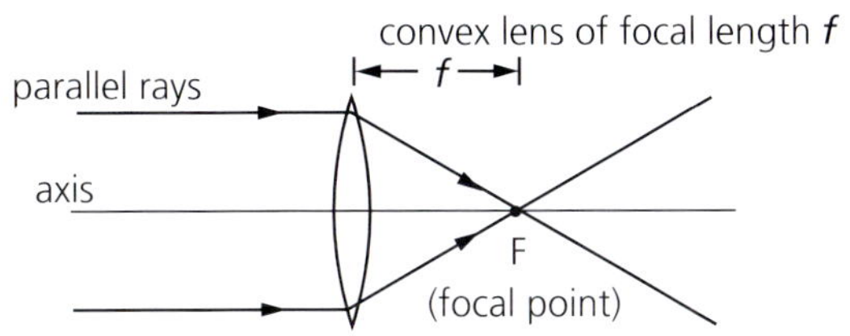


For a **concave lens** the focal point is where a parallel beam of light along the lens axis appears to spread out from.

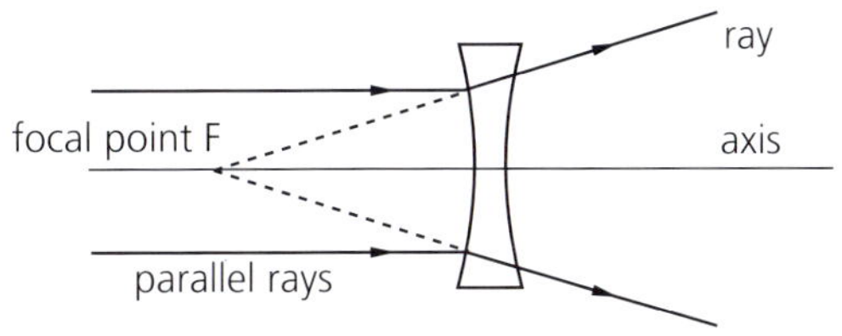


## Image formation by a convex lens

A **ray diagram** may be constructed to locate the position and size of the **image**. For a convex lens, two rays, ① and ② in the diagram below, are drawn from a point on the object. The image is formed where the two rays meet (a **real** image) or where they appear to come from (a **virtual** image).

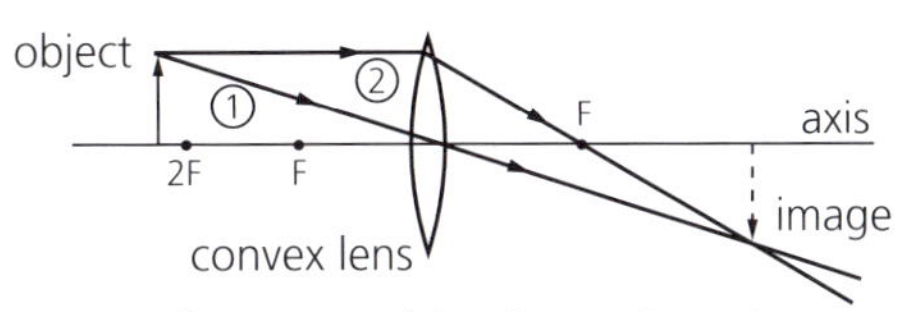


**The camera lens** – an object beyond 2F gives a real inverted image on the other side of the lens between F and 2F.

# The eye

- The eye lens and the cornea focus light from a point object onto a point on the retina.
- The retina is a layer of light-sensitive cells at the back of the eyeball. Cells stimulated by light send nerve impulses to the brain.
- The power of the eye lens is altered by the ciliary muscles which make the lens thicker when they contract.

## Sight correction

- **Long sight** is corrected using a convex lens, enabling near objects to be seen clearly.
- **Short sight** is corrected using a concave lens which makes parallel light diverge, enabling distant objects to be seen clearly.

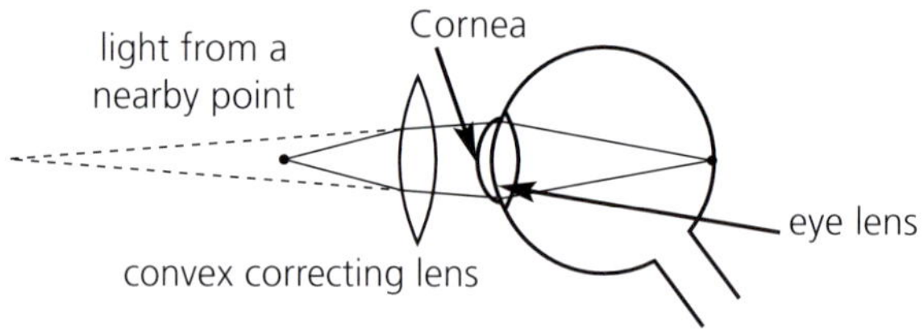


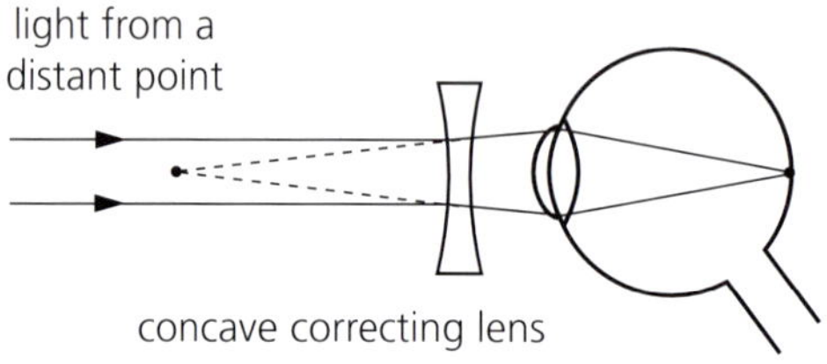


### The eye

The cornea helps to focus light onto the retina, acting like a 'fixed focus' lens.

The eye lens provides an 'adjustable focus' lens.

# The camera

- In a camera, the **lens position** is adjusted so that the image of the object is in focus on the film.
- Usually, the object is beyond 2F, so the lens forms a diminished inverted real image on the film which is between F and 2F on the other side of the lens.
- If the object is at infinity, the image is formed in the same plane as the focal point of the lens.

## Ray diagram for a camera

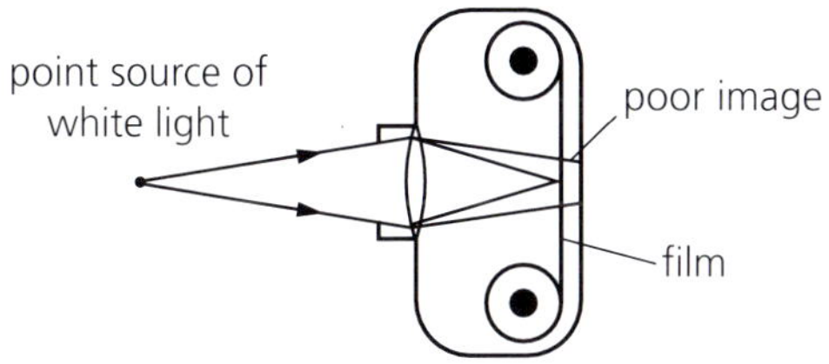


- The lens position needs to be changed to keep the image in focus on the film if the object position changes.
- To photograph a nearer object the lens must be moved away from the film.
- In a simple camera the image may be tinged with colour because white light is split into the colours of the spectrum by the lens. (See p. 32.)

### Quick quiz

1. What does a convex lens do to a parallel beam of light?
2. What adjustment is made to a camera to take photographs of objects at different distances?
3. How does the eye adjust itself to see objects at different distances?

**Answers**

1. Makes it converge to the focal point of the lens
2. The distance from the lens to the film needs to be adjusted
3. The eye lens is automatically made thinner to see objects clearly further away

# The electromagnetic spectrum

All electromagnetic waves travel through space at the same speed.

| **Radiation** | **Wavelength** | **Notes** |
|---|---|---|
| Radio waves | > 0.1 m | Reflected by metals |
| Microwaves | 0.1 mm to 0.1 m | Reflected by metals, transmitted and detected by concave dish aerials connected to suitable circuits |
| Infra-red radiation | 700 nm to 0.1 mm | Detected by an infra-red sensor or special photographic film or a blackened thermometer |
| Visible light | 400 nm (violet) to 700 nm (red) | Reflected by metals, absorbed by pigment molecules |
| Ultra-violet light | about 0.1 nm to 400 nm | Detected by photographic film, photocells, UV sensitive dyes, absorbed by the skin |
| X-rays and gamma rays | < 0.1 nm | X-rays are produced by X-ray tubes, gamma rays are produced by radioactive isotopes, detected by photographic film or Geiger tubes |

**Note**

1 mm = 0.001 m
1 nm = 0.000000001 m

# Uses of electromagnetic waves

## Communications

- Electromagnetic waves are used in radio and TV broadcasting, microwave beam communications and infra-red transmitters.
- A carrier wave is modulated to enable the signal carrying the information to be transmitted. The modulated carrier wave is detected by a receiver and the carrier wave is removed, leaving only the modulating signal.

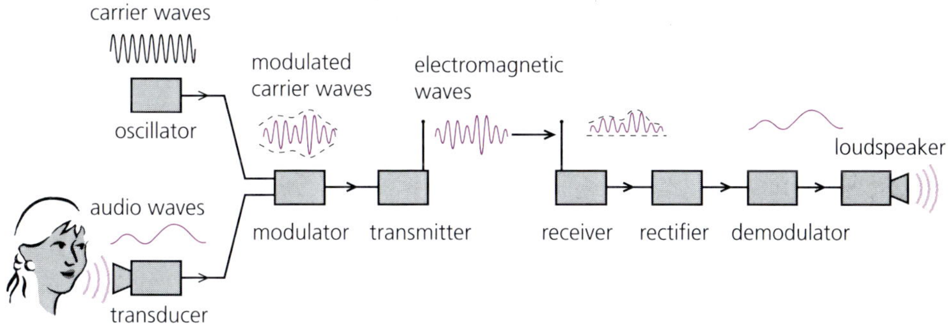


## Medical diagnosis and treatment of disorders

Visible light, X-rays and gamma rays are used as follows.

- Endoscopes are optical fibre devices used to see inside the body. (see p. 26).
- X-rays are used to form images of bones – X-rays from an X-ray tube pass through tissue and are absorbed by bones; the patient is placed between the tube and a film; X-rays blacken the film so a 'negative' image is formed on the film of any bones that block the path of the X-rays; certain internal organs (e.g. the stomach) are supplied with a 'contrast' medium that absorbs the X-rays.
- High energy X-ray beams and gamma ray beams are used to destroy tumours. The beam is directed into the patient at the tumour from different directions so that the surrounding healthy tissue is unaffected.

## Security

Examples include ultra-violet marker pens and infra-red detectors.

# Colour

## The visible spectrum

This can be produced by passing a narrow beam of white light through a prism. Note that red light bends least and violet light most. The splitting of white light into the colours of the spectrum is called **dispersion**.

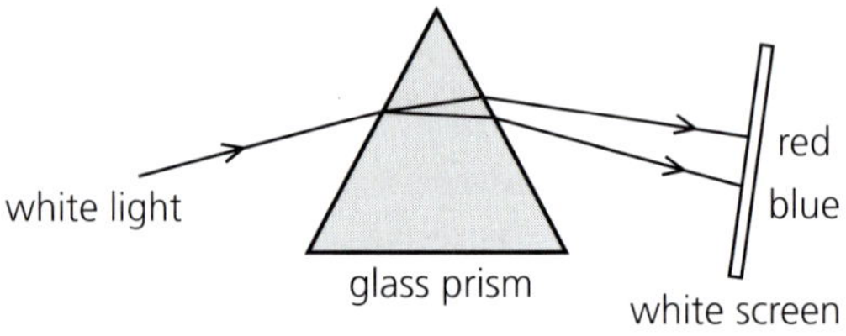


## Colour and wavelength

The wavelength of light varies according to its colour, from about 400 nm for blue light to about 700 nm for red light.

## The colour of a surface

Light incident on a surface which is not a mirror is either absorbed or scattered by the surface.

- A black surface absorbs all the light that falls on it.
- A white surface scatters all colours of light incident on it.
- A coloured surface seen in white light scatters light of that colour and absorbs all other colours – e.g. a blue surface in white light absorbs all colours of light except blue light.

### Quick quiz

1. Which colour of light, red or blue, has the longer wavelength?
2. What is the approximate wavelength of blue light?
3. Name the three primary colours of light.
4. Which two primary colours of light overlap to produce yellow light on a white screen?
5. What would be the colour of a red card in (a) blue light, (b) yellow light?

**Answers**

1. red
2. 400 nm
3. red, green, blue
4. red and green
5. (a) black, (b) red

# Waves quiz

## Questions

**1** State whether the following waves are transverse or longitudinal: (a) sound, (b) light.

**2** What is polarised light?

**3** What is the amplitude of a wave?

**4** State the equation relating the speed of a wave to its frequency and its wavelength.

**5** A water wave spreads out after passing through a gap. This is an example of which property of a wave?

**6** What determines the pitch of a sound?

**7** What are ultrasonic waves?

**8** Which type of seismic wave (a) creates most damage to buildings, (b) can pass through a liquid?

**9** What condition is essential for a light ray to undergo total internal reflection?

**10** (a) What properties of X-rays makes them suitable to take photos of internal organs? (b) What properties of microwaves makes them suitable for satellite communications?

### Answers

**1** (a) Longitudinal (b) transverse **2** Light waves that vibrate in one plane only **3** The distance from equilibrium to peak displacement (or the height from the centre for a transverse wave) **4** Speed = frequency x wavelength **5** Diffraction **6** The frequency of the sound waves **7** Sound waves of frequency above the upper frequency limit of the normal human ear **8** (a) L waves (b) P waves **9** The angle of incidence must exceed the critical angle **10** (a) X-rays penetrate tissue but not bone (b) microwaves pass through the atmosphere

# Energy, force and motion 3

## Energy transfer

- **Energy** is the capacity of a body to do work.
- **Work** is done when a force makes an object move.
- **Heat** is energy transferred where temperature differences exist.
- Energy exists in different forms and can be changed from any form into other forms.
- Forms of energy include chemical energy, elastic energy, electrical energy, kinetic energy, light, nuclear energy, potential energy, sound and thermal energy.
- The unit of energy is the **joule** (J). This is the work done when a force of 1 newton (N) moves through 1 metre.
- The **Principle of Conservation of Energy** states that whenever energy changes take place the total energy after the change is equal to the total energy before the change (conservation means 'staying the same').

### Energy equations:

- work done = force x distance moved in the direction of the force
- kinetic energy = ½ x mass x speed$^2$
- change of potential energy = mass x gravity x change of height.

### Conservation of energy

'Conservation' means staying the same. When energy is used, the total amount of energy after it has been used is the same as before it was used.

Energy is measured in joules (J). One joule of energy is used when 1 newton of force moves its point of application through 1 metre in the direction of the force.

Make sure you learn the energy equations and how to use them. Don't forget to include g when you work out a change of potential energy.

# Power and efficiency

- **Power** = rate of transfer of energy

$$= \frac{\text{energy transferred}}{\text{time taken}}$$

- The unit of power is the watt (W) equal to 1 joule per second; 1 kilowatt (kW) = 1000 watts.

- One kilowatt hour (kW h) is the energy supplied in 1 hour at a rate of transfer of 1 kilowatt; note that 1 kW h = 3,600,000 joules ( = 1000 J/s x 3600 s).

- Electrical power (in watts) = current (in amperes) x voltage (in volts)

- Rearranging the power equation gives

$$\text{current} = \frac{\text{power}}{\text{voltage}}$$ or

$$\text{voltage} = \frac{\text{power}}{\text{current}}$$

- **Efficiency** of a machine =

$$\frac{\text{power output}}{\text{power input}} = \frac{\text{useful work done by the machine}}{\text{energy supplied to machine}}$$

- **Energy dissipated** = energy supplied to machine – useful work done by the machine (*dissipated means 'spread out'*).

- The causes of inefficiency of a machine include friction between moving parts, fluid resistance and electrical resistance. No machine is perfectly efficient.

- Example; an electric motor uses 100 J of electrical energy to increase the potential energy of a weight by 80 J. The other 20 J is dissipated due to mechanical friction and electrical heating.

# States of matter

All natural substances are formed from just 92 elements which cannot be broken down into other elements. The smallest particle of an element is an atom. A molecule is two or more atoms held together by strong bonds. An ion is a charged atom or molecule. A compound is a substance that contains elements in fixed proportions and consists of molecules or ions.

- In a **solid** the particles are locked together in contact with each other in a rigid structure.
- In a **liquid** the particles move about at random in contact with each other.
- In a **gas** the particles move about at random much further apart from each other than in a liquid or a solid. Most of a gas is empty space.
- **Temperature** is a measure of the hotness of an object.
- Absolute temperature (in kelvins) = Celsius temperature (°C) + 273.
- Absolute zero (= 0 kelvins = –273°C) is the lowest possible temperature.
- The **melting point** of a solid is the temperature at which it changes from a solid to a liquid.
- The **boiling point** of a liquid is the temperature at which it changes from a liquid to a vapour as a result of bubbles of vapour forming throughout the liquid.
- A **vapour** is a gas that can be liquefied by compression.

## Quick quiz

Fill in the missing words from the following list.

collide contact locked randomly spaced

1. In a solid, the particles are __________ together.
2. In a gas, the particles are __________ further apart than in a liquid or a solid. They move __________, making contact only when they __________.
3. In a liquid, the particles move about __________ in __________ with each other.

**Answers**

1. locked
2. spaced, randomly, collide
3. randomly, contact

# Energy resources

## Fuels

The World's fuel resources supply most of our energy needs at present. However, once a fuel has been used, it cannot be re-used. Renewable resources can however be re-used.

- **Fuels** release energy as a result of reactions changing the fuel into another substance.
- **Fossil fuels** include coal, oil, gas and wood.
- **Nuclear fuel** is obtained from natural uranium.

## Renewable energy

These resources supply energy without changing one substance into another.

- Solar radiation is absorbed by solar cells and solar panels.
- Indirect use of solar radiation includes hydroelectricity, wind power (i.e. aerogenerators) and wave power.
- Non-solar energy resources include geothermal power and tidal power.

### UK energy supplies

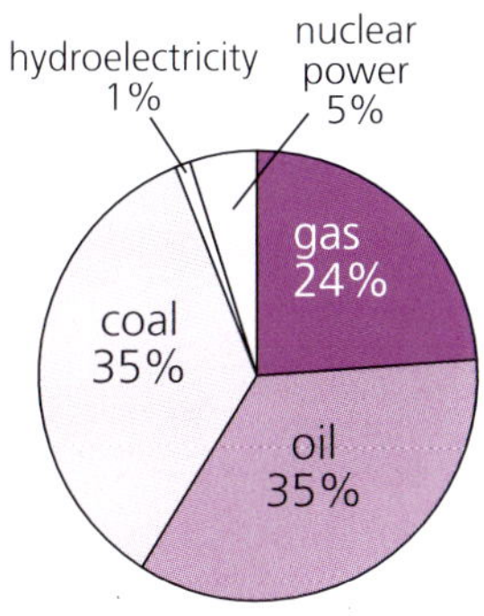


### UK energy demands

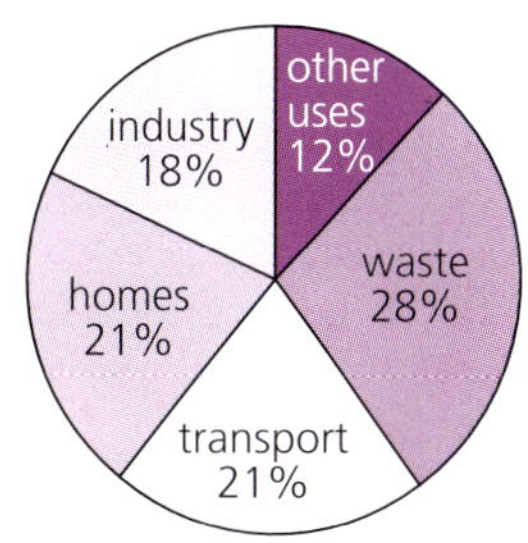


## Quick Quiz

Name 4 different fuels and 4 different renewable energy sources.

# Using energy resources more efficiently

**Consumers** could use energy more efficiently as follows:

- Make machines and vehicles more efficient (e.g. reduce friction between moving parts).
- Replace inefficient machines and vehicles.
- Reduce car usage, fit automatic lighting and thermostats in buildings.

**Producers** could reduce energy wastage as follows:

- Combined heat and power stations for district heating. Steam-driven turbines are used to drive a.c. generators in power stations. The thermal energy of the steam may be used to provide hot water to heat local buildings.
- Pumped storage of off-peak electricity. Nuclear power stations cannot be turned off when the demand for power is low. The electricity generated by nuclear power stations at times of low demand (off-peak electricity) is supplied to pumped-storage stations to pump water to high-level reservoirs. The pump turbines are reversible so that at times of high demand the flow of water is reversed and used to make the turbines generate electricity.

The world's reserves of oil and gas are unlikely to last beyond the 21st century. In the future, cars could burn hydrogen produced by electrolysis of water. The electricity for this process could come from solar power or another renewable resource.

## Checklist

1. List five different fuels, including one non-fossil fuel.
2. List five different renewable energy resources.
3. What is a combined heat and power station?
4. What is an aerogenerator?

**Answers**

1. and 2. See p. 37

3. steam used to drive the electricity generators is then used to heat local buildings instead of being wasted

4. a wind-driven turbine that is used to generate electricity

# Thermal energy

Thermal energy is the energy gained by a substance when its temperature rises or when it melts or when it vaporises.

- When a **solid** is heated and its temperature rises, its molecules vibrate more.
- When a solid is heated at its **melting point**, it becomes a liquid. Its particles (i.e. atoms or molecules or ions) break free from each other and move about in contact.
- When a **liquid** is heated and its temperature rises, its particles move about faster.
- When a liquid is heated at its **boiling point**, bubbles of vapour form throughout the liquid and rise to the surface. The particles break away from each other completely.
- The energy **needed** to melt a solid or vaporise a liquid is called **latent heat**. This energy is released as heat when a vapour condenses or a liquid solidifies.

## Thermal energy and temperature changes

- The temperature change of a substance when thermal energy is supplied or removed from it depends on the material (i.e. on the substance and its physical state).
- The **specific heat capacity** of a material is the energy needed to raise the temperature of 1 kg of a material by 1 K (i.e. 1°C).

*Example*

The specific heat capacity of water is 4200 J/kg/K. To heat 5 kg of water from 20°C to 100°C therefore requires 1.68 MJ of thermal energy (= 5 kg x 4200 J/kg/K x (100 – 20)°C.

*Note*

This type of calculation could appear at GCSE even if the term 'specific heat capacity' is not used.

# Heat transfer

- **Thermal conduction** occurs in solids, liquids and gases.
- Metals are the best conductors of heat. This is because they contain electrons that move about freely in the metal.
- Thermal insulators are poor conductors of heat because all the electrons are fixed to atoms.
- **Thermal convection** occurs only in liquids and gases. Convection occurs because hot liquid or gas rises and displaces the cold liquid or gas.

## Thermal convection in water

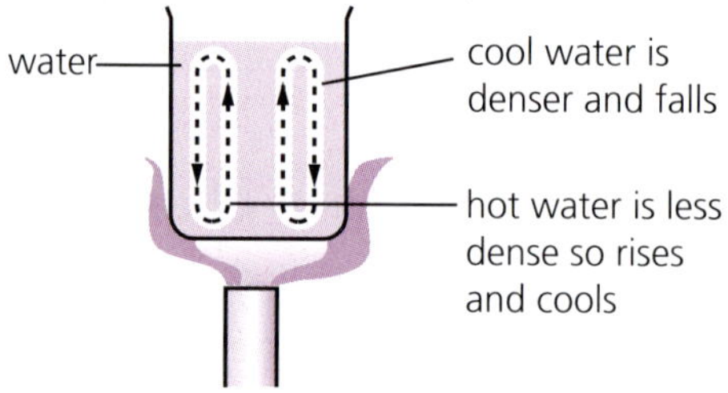


- **Thermal radiation** is electromagnetic radiation emitted from a surface.
- The hotter a surface is, the more thermal radiation it emits.
- A matt surface is a better emitter and absorber of thermal radiation than a smooth surface. A black surface is a better emitter and absorber of thermal radiation than a silvered surface.
- Thermal radiation can pass through a vacuum.
- **Evaporation** causes loss of thermal energy from a hot liquid in an open container.

### Note

Boiling and evaporation are not the same. Evaporation only takes place at the surface and increases with temperature.

Boiling only happens at the boiling point but takes place throughout the liquid.

# Evaporation

Evaporation is the process of a liquid **vaporising** below its boiling point. A liquid in an insulated open container **cools** because it vaporises. This is because the faster-moving molecules in the liquid escape so the average kinetic energy of the remaining liquid molecules decreases.

## The process of evaporation

**The more energetic molecules can escape from the surface of the liquid.** A molecule at the surface of the liquid must do work to overcome the attraction between it and the other molecules there. Only fast-moving molecules have sufficient kinetic energy to break free of these forces of attraction.

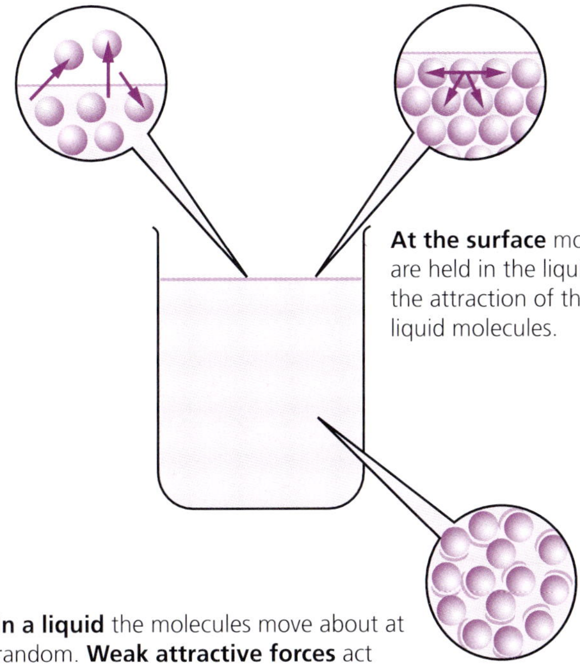

**At the surface** molecules are held in the liquid by the attraction of the other liquid molecules.

**In a liquid** the molecules move about at random. **Weak attractive forces** act between the molecules to keep them together.

# Controlling heat transfer

Think about conduction, convection and radiation in any heat transfer situation. If a liquid is present, add evaporation to your thoughts.

**Heat loss in the home** can be reduced by:

- fitting loft insulation to reduce thermal conduction through the roof
- fitting double glazing to reduce thermal conduction and convection
- installing cavity wall insulation to reduce thermal conduction through the walls
- placing metal foil between the radiators and the walls to reduce heat loss due to radiation
- closing the curtains to reduce radiation through the windows
- fitting draught excluders round the external doors to reduce thermal convection
- fitting an insulation jacket round a hot water tank. This reduces heat loss because the insulation jacket is a very poor thermal conductor.

**Heat loss from an engine** can be **increased** by fan-assisted cooling to increase convection, painting the engine black to increase radiation and by fitting cooling fins to increase the surface area and hence increase convection and radiation.

## Heat

Home heating bills can be reduced by low-cost measures such as placing metal foil behind a wall radiator and closing the curtains. Both measures reduce heat loss due to thermal radiation.

In addition, fitting an insulation jacket to the hot water tank reduces heat loss from the tank. The insulation jacket reduces thermal conduction to the outer surface of the tank.

With an insulation jacket fitted, the outermost surface of the tank is cooler so heat losses due to thermal radiation and thermal convection are reduced considerably.

# Energy and force quiz

## Questions

**1** State the unit of (i) energy, (ii) force.

**2** How much work is done when a weight of 5 N is raised through a height of 2 m?

**3** Calculate the kinetic energy of an object of mass 3 kg moving at a speed of 4 m/s.

**4** How much energy is supplied to a 100 W light bulb in 1 minute when it is switched on?

**5** Why is a gas in general much less dense than a solid?

**6** Why must energy be supplied to a solid to melt it?

**7** Why is a metal a good conductor of electricity?

**8** Which form of heat loss from a home in winter is reduced as a result of drawing the curtains over a window?

**9** Name three different renewable energy resources.

**10** What is a pumped storage power station?

### Answers

**1** (i) The joule (ii) The newton **2** 10 J **3** 24 J **4** 6000 J **5** There are large spaces between the particles in a gas whereas the particles in a solid are in contact with each other **6** To enable the particles of the solid to break the bonds that lock them together **7** It contains electrons that move about freely inside the metal **8** Thermal radiation **9** See p. 37 **10** See p. 38

# Speed and velocity

- **Speed** is distance moved per unit time.
- **Velocity** is speed in a given direction.
- Speed (in m/s) = $\frac{\text{distance moved (in m)}}{\text{time taken (in s)}}$

## Distance v time graphs

The gradient of a distance v time graph = speed.

- For **constant** speed, the gradient is a straight line. The greater the speed, the steeper the line.

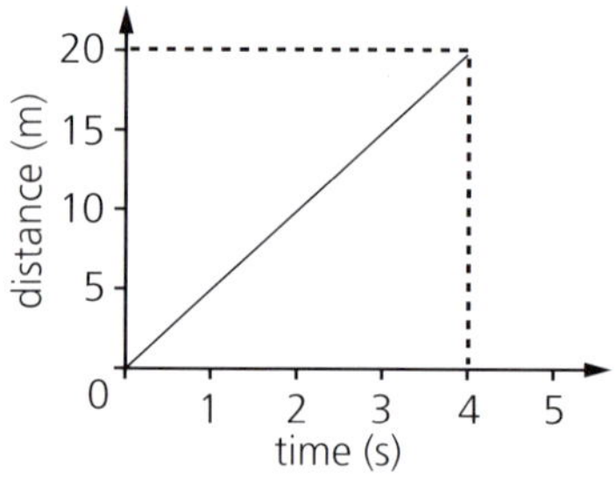


- For **changing** speed, the gradient of the line at any point is the speed at that point.

## Increasing speed

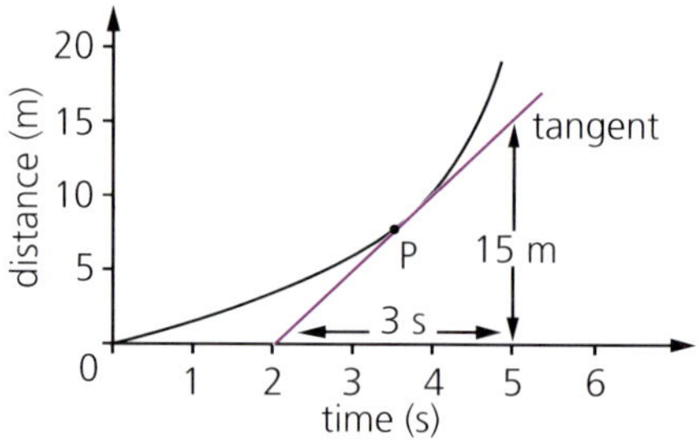


The speed at P = $\frac{15\text{ m}}{3\text{ s}}$ = 5 m/s.

# Acceleration

Acceleration is change of velocity per unit time.

$$\text{Acceleration (m/s}^2\text{)} = \frac{\text{change of velocity (in m/s)}}{\text{time taken (in s)}}$$

## Speed v time graphs

For **constant acceleration**:

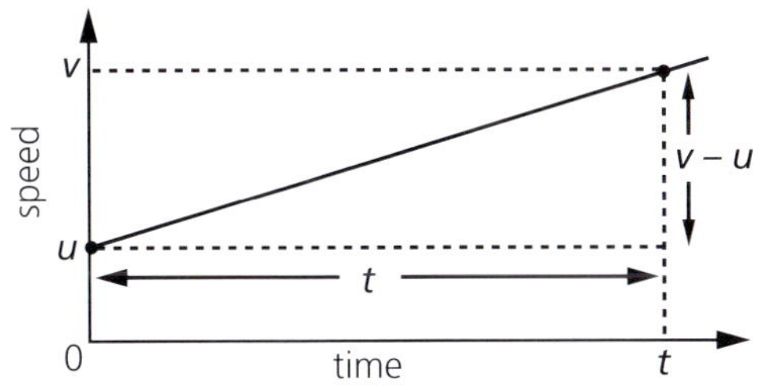


- the gradient of a speed v time graph = acceleration (= (v – u)/t on the graph)
- the area under a speed v time graph = the distance moved (= $\frac{1}{2}$(u + v)t on the graph)
- the word 'uniform' meaning 'the same' is sometimes used instead of 'constant'.

For **changing acceleration**:

- the gradient of a speed v time graph at any point = acceleration at that point
- the area under a speed v time graph = the distance moved.

## Acceleration due to gravity

An object near the Earth's surface acted on only by gravity experiences a constant acceleration vertically downwards. The value of this acceleration, denoted by g, is approximately 10 m/$s^2$.

# Stopping distances

- **Stopping distance** = thinking distance + braking distance.
- **Thinking distance** = distance moved by the vehicle in the time it takes the driver to react.
- During the thinking time the vehicle is moving at constant speed so the thinking distance is proportional to the speed.
- **Braking distance** = distance moved by the vehicle from the point where the brakes are applied to where it stops.
- During the braking time the vehicle decelerates. The faster an object is travelling before the brakes are applied, the longer it takes to stop and the greater its average speed. The braking distance is therefore proportional to the square of the initial speed.

## Distance – speed graphs for a braking car

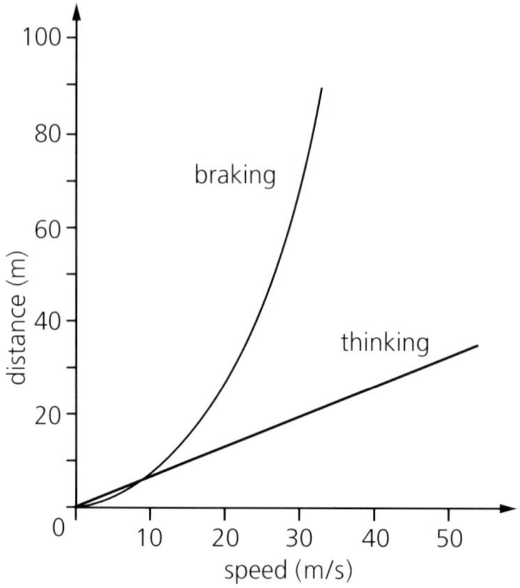


**React . . . Brake . . . Stop**

In that order

# Force and acceleration

## Newton's laws of motion

- **1st Law** An object continues at rest or in uniform motion unless acted on by a force.
- **2nd Law** For an object of constant mass which is acted on by a resultant force (i.e. an overall force)

| **Force** | = | **mass** | x | **acceleration** |
|---|---|---|---|---|
| (in newtons) | | (in kg) | | (in $m/s^2$) |

- **3rd Law** When two objects interact, they exert equal and opposite forces on each other.
- One newton is defined as the force necessary to give a mass of 1 kg an acceleration of 1 $m/s^2$.

## Weight

The weight of an object is the force of gravity on it. Since an object acted on by gravity alone experiences constant acceleration g, the force of gravity on it equals its mass x g.

| **Weight** | = | **mass** | x | **g** |
|---|---|---|---|---|
| (in newtons) | | (in kg) | | (in $m/s^2$) |

## Terminal speed

An object released from rest in a fluid reaches a constant speed referred to as its **terminal speed**. At this speed, the 'drag' force due to the fluid is equal and opposite to the weight of the object so there is no resultant force on the object and its acceleration is zero. A parachutist descending at constant speed is acted on by an upward drag force equal and opposite to his or her total weight.

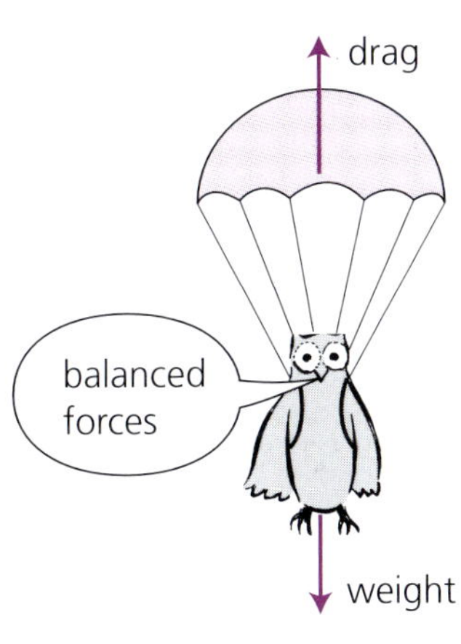

# Work, energy and power reminders

## Definitions

- **Work** is done when a force is used to move an object.
- **Energy** is the capacity of a body to do work.
- **Power** is the rate of transfer of energy.

## Equations

- Work (in J) = force (in N) x distance moved in the direction of the force (in m).

- $$\text{Power (in W)} = \frac{\text{energy transferred (in J)}}{\text{time taken (in s)}}$$

- Change of potential energy = mass x g x change of height.

- Kinetic energy = $\frac{1}{2}$ x mass x speed$^2$.

*Example*

$g = 10\ \text{m/s}^2$

A cyclist of mass 50 kg descended a steady incline of height 45 m from a standing start. The cyclist's speed at the foot of the incline was 15 m/s. Calculate (a) (i) the loss of potential energy of the cyclist, (ii) the cyclist's gain of kinetic energy down the incline, and (b) account for the difference between the loss of potential energy and the gain of kinetic energy.

**Solution** (a) (i) Loss of p.e. = mass x g x height change = 50 x 10 x 45 = 22 500 J (ii) Gain of k.e. = $\frac{1}{2}$ x mass x speed$^2$ = $\frac{1}{2}$ x 50 x 225 = 5625 J (b) The gain of k.e. is less than the loss of p.e. because energy is dissipated due to air resistance and friction.

### Quick quiz

Fill in the missing words in the equations below.

1. Work = force x _______________.
2. Kinetic energy = $\frac{1}{2}$ x mass x __________.
3. ______________ = energy/time
4. Change of potential energy = mass x g x _______________.
5. A steel ball released in water accelerates until its speed is ______________ . At this speed, it is acted on by a drag force which is _______________ to its weight.

**Answers**

1. distance
2. speed$^2$
3. power
4. change of height
5. constant, equal and opposite

# Equilibrium

## Balanced forces

If an object which is acted upon by several forces is in equilibrium (i.e. at rest), the forces must 'balance' each other out to give an overall force (the 'resultant') of zero. For example, an object acted on by two forces is in equilibrium only if the two forces are equal and act in opposite directions on the object. If the **resultant force** on an object is not zero, the object is accelerated in the direction of the resultant force. The forces acting on an object are said to be '**balanced**' if their overall effect is zero.

## Equal and opposite forces

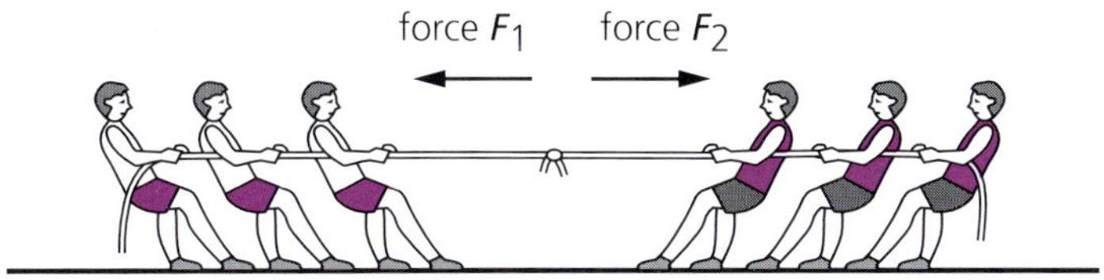


In tug-of-war 'stalemate', the teams pull with equal and opposite forces. The forces balance each other out $F_1 = F_2$

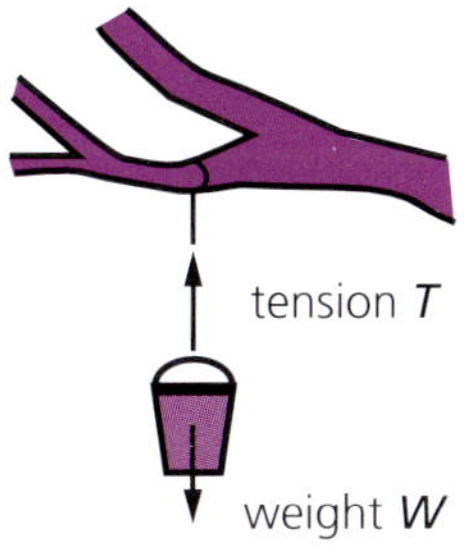


The weight of an object hanging on the end of a vertical rope is equal and opposite to the tension in the rope. $T = W$

## Centre of gravity

The centre of gravity of an object is the point where its weight may be considered to act. The centre of gravity of a freely-suspended object in equilibrium will always be directly under the point of suspension.

# Moments

- The **moment of a force about a point** = force x perpendicular distance from the point to the line of action of the force.
- The **Principle of Moments** states that for a body in equilibrium, the sum of the clockwise moments about any point = the sum of the anticlockwise moments about that point.

## Equal and opposite moments

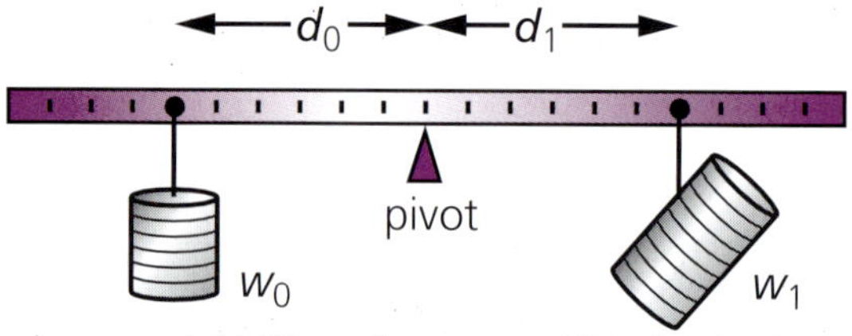


The unknown weight $W_1$ can be measured by adjusting its distance from the pivot until the rule is balanced. The moment of $W_1$= the moment of the known weight $W_0$.

$$W_0 d_0 = W_1 d_1$$

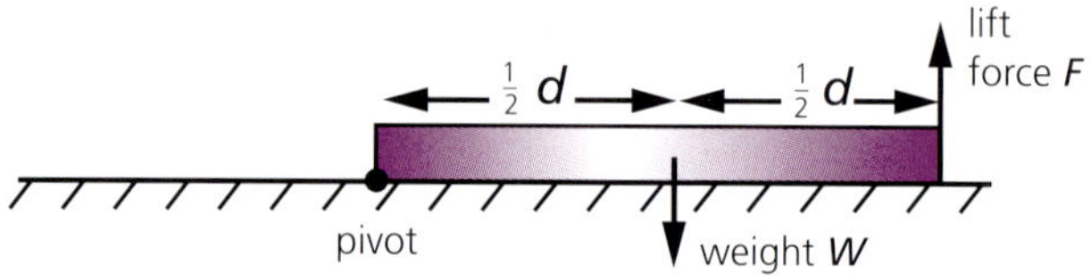


The force $F$ required to lift the concrete post at one end is half the weight $W$. This is because the moment of this force about the pivot must be at least equal to the moment of the weight about the pivot.

$$Fd = \frac{1}{2} dW$$

# Force and motion quiz

## Questions

1 How far does a vehicle moving at a steady speed of 20 m/s move in 1 minute?

2 Define acceleration and state its unit.

3 What feature of a speed v time graph gives the distance moved?

4 What does the gradient of a speed v time graph represent?

5 What is the thinking distance of a driver?

6 State the equation relating force, mass and acceleration.

7 The weight of a 1 kg mass at the Earth's surface is 10 N. Calculate the weight of a 70 kg person at this position.

8 Calculate the resultant force needed to make a vehicle of mass 600 kg accelerate from rest to a speed of 10 m/s in 60 s.

9 Define the moment of a force about a point.

10 State the Principle of Moments.

**Answers**

**1** 1200 m **2** Change of velocity/time taken; $m/s^2$ **3** The area under the line **4** The acceleration **5** Distance travelled at constant speed in the time it takes the driver to react **6** Force = mass x acceleration **7** 700 N **8** 100 N **9** Force x perpendicular distance from the line of action of the force to the point **10** For a body in equilibrium the sum of the clockwise moments about any point = the sum of the anticlockwise moments about that point

## Hooke's law

- A stretched spring will return to its original length if the forces used to stretch it are removed.
- The **extension** of the spring is the increase of length from its original length.
- The **tension** in the spring acts to return it to its original length. At any given extension the tension is equal and opposite to the force used to stretch the spring.
- **Hooke's law states that the extension of a spring is proportional to the force used to stretch it.**

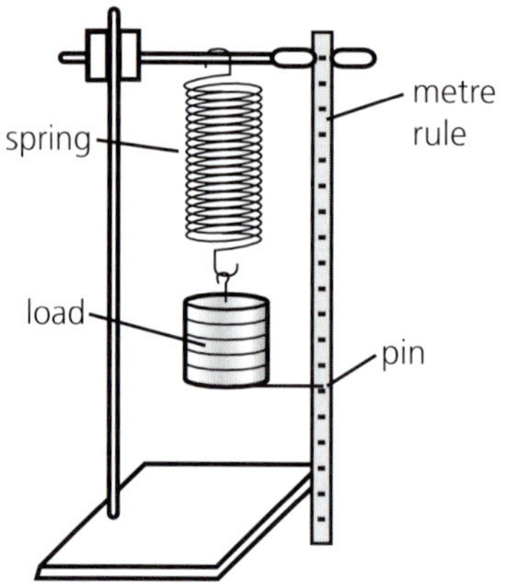


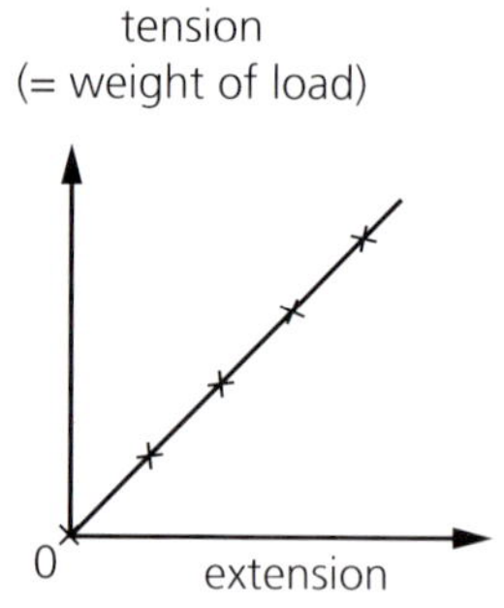


- A graph of tension v extension is a straight line through the origin.
- Equation for Hooke's law: Hooke's law can be written as an equation in the form $T = ke$, where $T$ is the tension in the spring, $e$ is the extension and $k$ is a constant that depends on the spring.

# Elastic and plastic behaviour

A solid has a definite shape because its particles are held together by strong bonds. The shape of a solid can be changed by applying forces to it. The diagrams below show how the extension of objects made of different materials changes with force.

- **Elastic behaviour** of a material is its ability to regain its shape after removal of the forces that deformed it.
- The **elastic limit** of a solid is the limit of its ability to regain its shape. Beyond its elastic limit, it deforms permanently.
- **Plastic behaviour** occurs when the shape of an object is permanently changed by external forces.

## Stretching materials

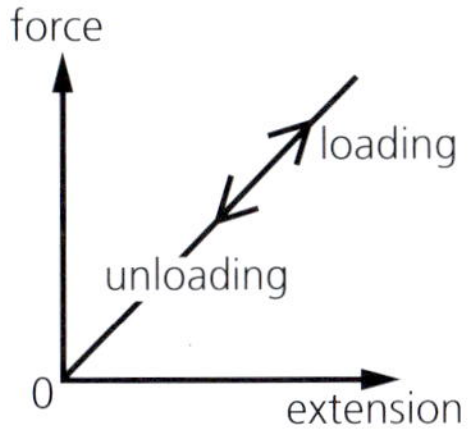


A spring obeys Hooke's law up to a limit referred to as its 'limit of proportionality'. For steel, this limit and the elastic limit are very close.

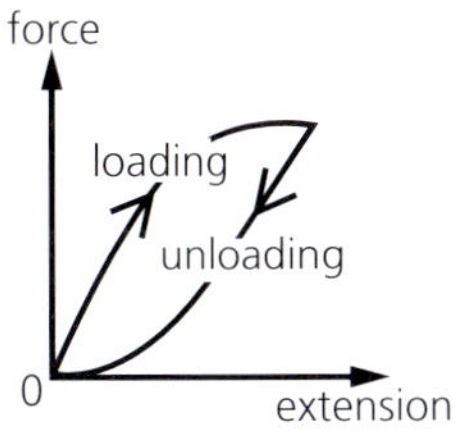


An elastic band does not obey Hooke's law, but it regains its original length so it is elastic.

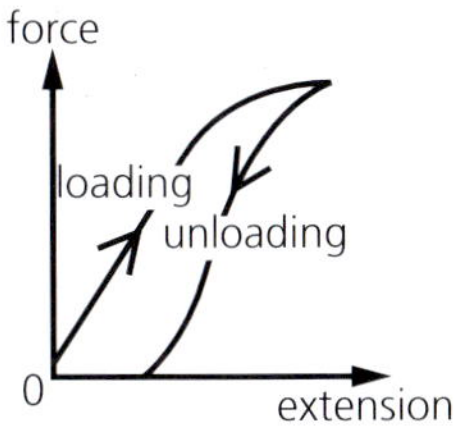


A polythene strip has a very low elastic limit and is easily stretched permanently.

# Density

$$\text{Density} = \frac{\text{mass}}{\text{volume}}$$

$$\text{Mass} = \text{volume} \times \text{density}$$

$$\text{Volume} = \frac{\text{mass}}{\text{density}}$$

## Units

- Mass – kilograms (kg).
- Volume – cubic metres ($m^3$).
- Density – kilogram per cubic metre ($kg/m^3$).

## Density measurements

- **Solids** – use a top pan balance to measure the mass of the solid, measure its volume by placing it in a suitably-filled measuring cylinder or displacement can. Measure the increase of volume which is equal to the volume of the solid. Use the density formula to calculate the density.
- **Liquids** – use a top pan balance to measure the mass of a measuring cylinder with and without the liquid in it. The difference between the readings is the mass of the liquid. Measure the volume of liquid in the measuring cylinder directly and use the density formula to calculate the density.
- **Gas** – measure the mass of a sealed flask of known volume containing the gas; pump the gas out using a vacuum pump and measure the mass of the empty flask. The difference between the readings is the mass of the gas; use the density formula to calculate the density.

## Using a displacement can

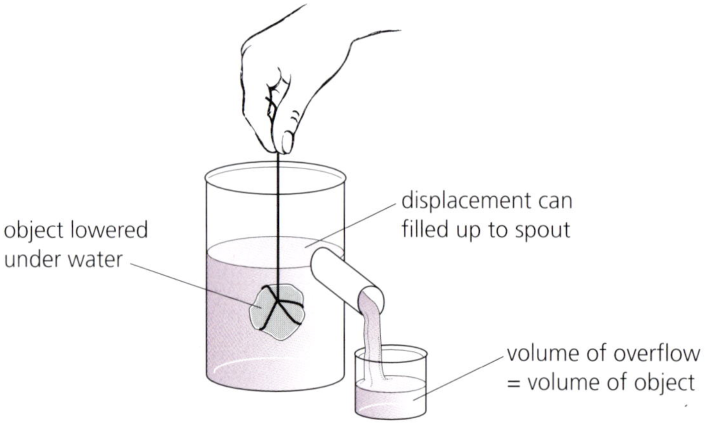

# Pressure

$$\textbf{Pressure (in pascals or N/m}^2\textbf{)} = \frac{\textbf{force (in N)}}{\textbf{area (in m}^2\textbf{)}}$$

Rearranging the pressure equation gives

force = pressure x area, or

$$\text{area} = \frac{\text{force}}{\text{pressure}}$$

### For two solids in contact the pressure is:

- greater, the smaller the area of contact (e.g. knife edge, needle)
- smaller, the larger the area of contact (e.g. caterpillar tracks, snow shoes).

### The pressure in a liquid at rest:

- acts in all directions
- increases with depth
- is the same along a horizontal line
- increases with the density of the liquid.

### The pressure in a gas:

- is due to gas molecules repeatedly hitting the sides of the container
- increases if the gas temperature is increased because the molecules hit the sides more often and more forcefully
- increases in accordance with Boyle's law if the volume of the gas is decreased at constant temperature. This is because the molecules hit the sides of the container more often.
- **Boyle's law** states that for a fixed mass of gas at constant temperature

**pressure** x **volume** = **constant**.

**Note**

The bigger the pressure, the smaller the volume. The smaller the pressure, the bigger the volume. If p goes up, V goes down etc. etc.

# Pressure measurement

## Gas pressure

Bourdon gauge – this consists of a curved hollow metal tube. When pressure is applied to the gas in the tube, the tube becomes a little straighter. The movement of the end of the tube is used to make a pointer move across a calibrated scale.

## U tube manometer

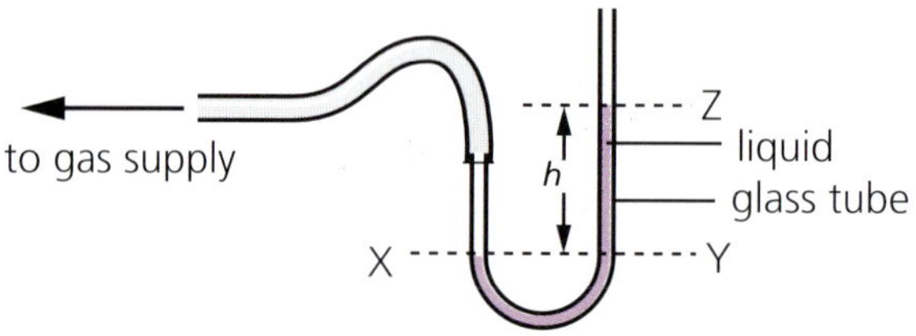


- the pressure at X is due to the gas supply
- the pressure at Y is due to the liquid column and the atmospheric pressure at Z
- the pressure at X is equal to the pressure at Y because X and Y are on the same level. The height of the liquid column is therefore a measure of how much the gas pressure exceeds atmospheric pressure.

## Atmospheric pressure

The pressure of the atmosphere decreases with height and changes slightly with the weather conditions.

## An aneroid barometer

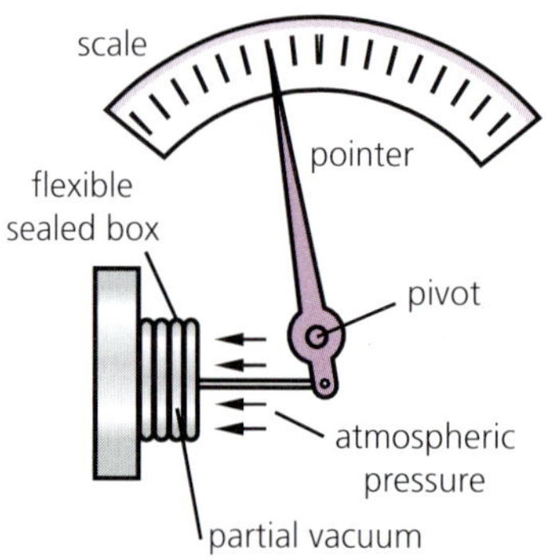


If the pressure of the atmosphere increases, the pointer moves to the right across the scale because the flexible box is squeezed.

# Hydraulics 1

A hydraulic system is used to increase the effect of a force. This is achieved by making the force act on a narrow piston to increase the pressure in a sealed liquid. The liquid pressure acts via a pipe on a large piston which exerts a much larger force than the force applied to the narrow piston.

## The hydraulic press

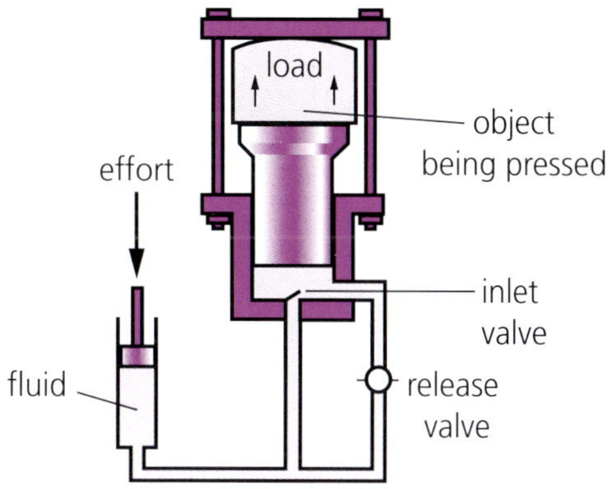


- The **pressure** in the liquid due to the narrow piston

$$= \frac{\text{force applied to the narrow piston}}{\text{area of the narrow piston}}$$

- The force exerted by the wide piston
  = pressure in the liquid x area of the wide piston.
- For example, if the area of the wide piston = 100 x the area of the narrow piston, the force exerted by the wide piston must therefore be 100 x the force applied to the narrow piston.
- Air in a hydraulic system reduces the increase of force because the pressure on the liquid is not fully transmitted to the wide piston.

# Hydraulics 2

## Vehicle brakes

In a vehicle brake system, a large force is exerted on the wheels as a result of a much smaller force being applied to the foot pedal.

## Disc brakes

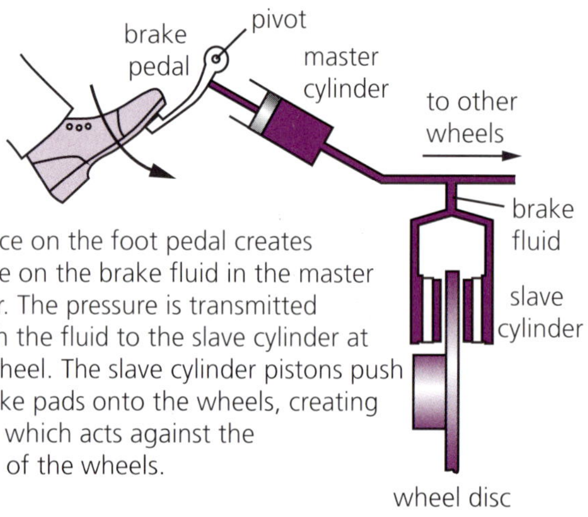


The force on the foot pedal creates pressure on the brake fluid in the master cylinder. The pressure is transmitted through the fluid to the slave cylinder at each wheel. The slave cylinder pistons push the brake pads onto the wheels, creating friction which acts against the motion of the wheels.

## A hydraulic car jack

This is used to raise a car wheel off the ground. The effort is repeatedly applied to raise the car body. A ratchet is used to ensure the car wheel remains raised each time the effort is applied.

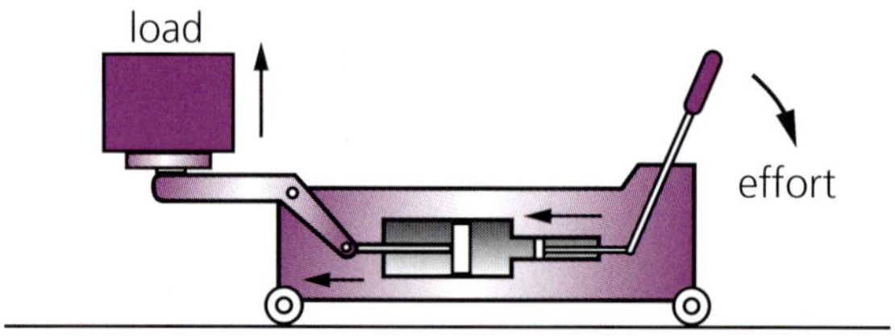

# Materials quiz

## Questions

**1** State Hooke's law.

**2** An unstretched spring has a length of 200 mm. One end of it is attached to a fixed point and a 2 N weight is hung on the other end. When the weight is at rest, the length of the spring is 300 mm.

(a) Calculate the extension of the spring when it supports the 2 N weight at rest.

(b) Calculate the weight needed to stretch it to a length of 400 mm.

**3** Sketch a graph to show how the extension of a rubber band changes with tension.

**4** An object of mass 400 kg has a volume of 0.05$m^3$. Calculate its density.

**5** Calculate the pressure exerted by a force of 40 N acting over an area of 0.1 $m^2$.

**6** Why does a sharp knife cut better than a blunt one?

**7** Why does the pressure in a gas increase if the gas is compressed without change of temperature?

**8** What is the purpose of a bourdon gauge?

**9** In a hydraulic brake system, why is the force on the wheels due to the brake pads much greater than the force on the brake pedal when the brakes are applied?

### Answers

**1** The extension of a spring is proportional to the force used to stretch it
**2** (a) 100 mm (b) 4 N **3** See p. 53 **4** 8000 kg/$m^3$ **5** 400 Pa **6** The sharper the blade the smaller the area of material it acts on so the greater the pressure it exerts on the material for a given force **7** The gas molecules hit the sides of the container more frequently **8** To measure the pressure of a gas **9** The brake pedal force acts on a narrow piston creating high pressure in the fluid. The fluid pressure acts on a wide piston at each wheel, creating a force on each wheel much greater than the brake pedal force

# Radioactivity

## Inside the atom

Every atom contains a positively charged nucleus consisting of **protons** and **neutrons**. **Electrons** are negatively charged particles that orbit the nucleus. An uncharged atom has an equal number of protons and electrons. Atoms with the same number of protons and different numbers of neutrons are **isotopes** of the same element.

## Isotopes

An isotope is defined by the symbol ${}^{A}_{Z}X$ where Z is the number of protons and A, the mass number, is the number of neutrons and protons. X is the chemical symbol for the element.

## Unstable nuclei

Most nuclei are stable. An unstable nucleus emits one of three types of radiation:

- **alpha radiation** ($\alpha$) consists of identical particles emitted by nuclei with too many neutrons and protons. An alpha particle consists of 2 protons and 2 neutrons
- **beta radiation** ($\beta$) consists of electrons which are emitted by nuclei with too many neutrons. A beta particle is created and emitted when a neutron in the nucleus changes into a proton
- **gamma radiation** ($\gamma$) is electromagnetic radiation emitted when a nucleus has emitted an alpha or beta particle and still has excess energy.

### Note

Protons are positive, neutrons are neutral and electrons are negative. The nucleus of an atom consists of neutrons and protons. Electrons orbit the nucleus.

The mass of a proton is about the same as the mass of a neutron. Electrons are much lighter. Atoms with the same number of protons and different numbers of neutrons are isotopes of the same element.

Radioactivity is due to unstable nuclei. The nuclei of a radioactive isotope become stable by emitting one of three types of radiation; alpha radiation, beta radiation or gamma radiation.

# $\alpha$, $\beta$ and $\gamma$ radiation

## Ionisation

An ion is formed from an uncharged atom as a result of:

- adding an electron to the atom (making it a negative ion because the number of protons in the nucleus is less than the number of electrons in the atom)
- removing an electron from the atom (making a positive ion because the number of protons in the nucleus now exceeds the number of electrons in the atom).

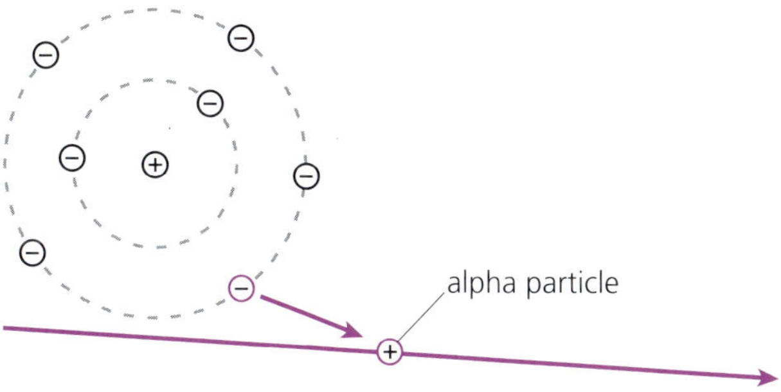


## Properties of $\alpha$, $\beta$ and $\gamma$ radiation

| | $\alpha$ | $\beta$ | $\gamma$ |
|---|---|---|---|
| Charge | +2e | –e | 0 |
| Absorption | Tissue paper | Few mm of aluminium | Several cm of lead |
| Range in air | Constant for a given isotope, no more than about 100 mm | Variable up to about 1 m | Spreads without limit |
| Ionising ability | Strong | Weak | Very weak |

Note

e = the magnitude of the charge of the electron.

## Equations for radioactive change

- $\alpha$-decay $\;{}^{A}_{Z}X \rightarrow {}^{4}_{2}\alpha + {}^{A-4}_{Z-2}Y$
- $\beta$-decay $\;{}^{A}_{Z}X \rightarrow {}^{0}_{-1}\beta + {}^{A}_{Z+1}Y$

# Radioactivity measurements

## Using a Geiger counter

In the diagram the Geiger tube is connected to a counter, the tube is sealed and contains a gas at low pressure. The thin window at the end of the tube is necessary to allow $\alpha$ **and** $\beta$ **radiation** to enter the tube. Every time an **ionising particle** enters the tube, the gas atoms in the tube are ionised and the gas conducts, allowing a pulse of electrons to pass through the counter to increase the count by one. The count rate from a radioactive source (i.e. the number of counts per second) is measured as follows.

- Measure the number of counts in a measured time with the tube at a fixed distance from the source.
- Calculate the uncorrected count rate which is the number of counts ÷ time taken.
- To correct for background radioactivity, measure the count rate with no source present. Subtract the background count rate from the uncorrected count rate to give the count rate due to the source only.

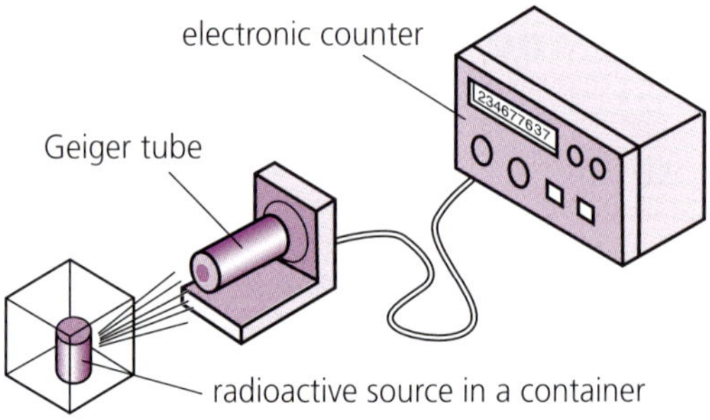


### Note

Ions are charged atoms. Ions are created by either removing electrons from, or adding electrons to, a neutral atom. Atoms are ionised by radiation from radioactive substances.

A Geiger counter consists of a Geiger tube connected to an electronic counter. Each time an alpha or a beta particle passes into the tube, the counter increases by one count.

Background radioactivity is due to radiation from radioactive substances in buildings and rocks. In addition, radiation from space, called cosmic radiation, causes background radioactivity.

# Radioactive decay

- The **activity** of a radioactive isotope is the number of disintegrations per second. The unit of activity is the **becquerel** (**Bq**).
- The **half-life** of a radioactive isotope is the time taken for the activity to decrease by half. This is the same as the time taken for the number of atoms of the radioactive isotope to decrease by half.

Note: in n half-lives the activity decreases to $\frac{1}{2^n}$ of the initial activity.

## Decay curves

If the activity of a radioactive isotope is plotted against time the result is a decay curve from which the half-life can be estimated. Since the activity of a radioactive isotope is proportional to the number of atoms of the isotope, a graph of the number of atoms v time for a radioactive isotope is also a decay curve.

## A decay curve

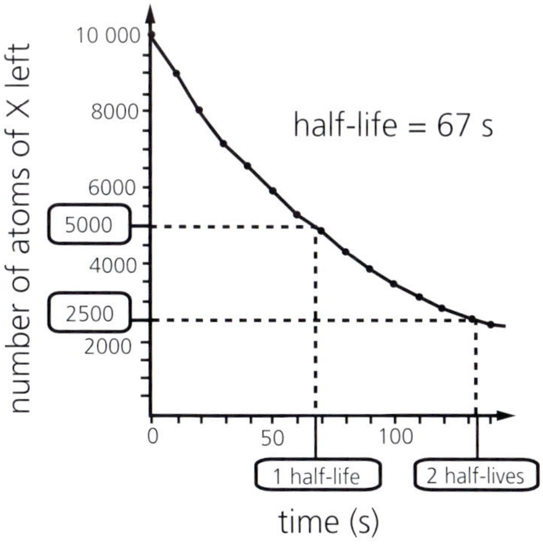


### Question

How many atoms would be left after 4 half-lives?

**Answer**

625

# Uses of radioactive isotopes

The choice of a suitable radioactive isotope for a particular application depends on:

- the **half-life** of the isotope
- the **type** of radiation emitted
- whether or not the **isotope** produced by the decay is **stable**
- the **ease of production** of the isotope.

## Industrial uses

### Radioactive tracers

Underground pipeline cracks can be detected by inserting a suitable radioactive isotope into the fluid flowing through the pipe. A Geiger counter is then moved at ground level along the length of the pipeline. Its reading shows an increase where fluid has leaked out of the pipe.

### Thickness monitoring of metal foil production

A $\beta$-emitting isotope is fixed on one side of the foil which is produced in a continuous strip. A Geiger counter is placed adjacent to the source on the other side of the foil. If the foil becomes thinner as it rolls off the production line, the counter reading increases and triggers a feedback mechanism to increase the foil thickness.

### Gamma irradiation

This is used to kill the bacteria responsible for food poisoning in certain foods. This makes the food safer to eat and prolongs its shelf life. Medical instruments are also sterilised using gamma irradiation. See p. 65 for uses of radioactive isotopes in medicine.

# Uses of radioactive isotopes in medicine

## Gamma therapy

A narrow beam of $\gamma$ **radiation** from radioactive **cobalt** is directed at a **tumour** from different directions to destroy the tumour. The cobalt source is in a thick lead container with a narrow hole to allow radiation out. Radioactive cobalt is used as it has a long half-life and produces high energy $\gamma$ radiation.

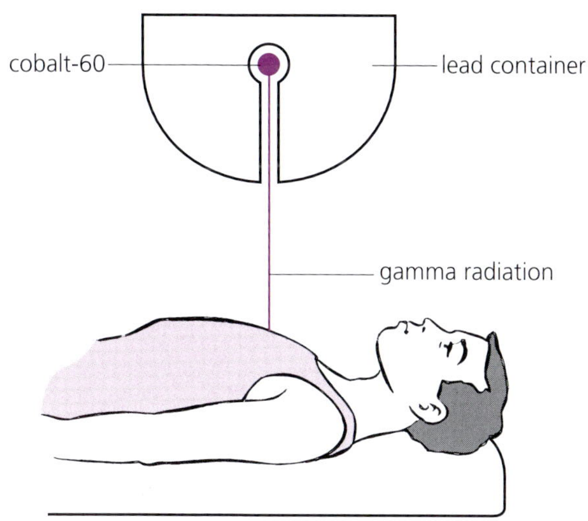


## Radioactive tracers in medicine

A suitable **radioactive isotope** in a solution is supplied to a patient either as a drink or by injection into a blood vessel. A Geiger counter is used to detect where the tracer goes. The isotope is a **$\beta$ or $\gamma$-emitter** with a half-life not too short (or it decays before it reaches the organ) and not too long (or it remains radioactive in the body).

- A **thyroid test** is used to find out if a thyroid gland is underactive. Iodine is absorbed by the thyroid gland. By supplying the patient with a small quantity of radioactive iodine, the uptake of iodine by the gland can be monitored by means of a Geiger counter held near the gland.
- A **blocked kidney** can be detected by supplying the patient with a drink containing a small quantity of **radioactive iodine**. The reading of a Geiger counter held near the kidney is monitored. If the reading increases and does not decrease, the solution has entered, but not left, the kidney so the kidney must be blocked.

# Nuclear fission

A uranium 235 ($^{235}_{92}U$) nucleus splits into two fragments when struck by a slow-moving neutron, releasing two or three neutrons in the process. The fragments and the neutrons fly apart, carrying away kinetic energy. The neutrons can cause **further fission** to maintain a chain of fission reactions.

## Fission

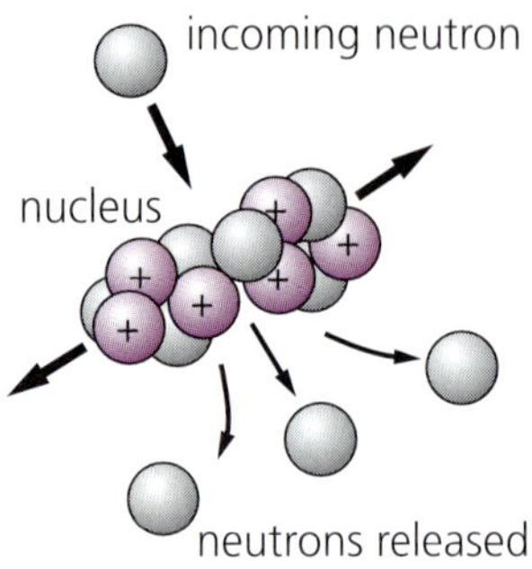


- To maintain a steady chain reaction (and therefore a steady rate of release of energy), exactly one neutron per fission on average must go on to produce further fission. This condition is achieved in a nuclear reactor by using control rods to absorb surplus neutrons.
- A nuclear reactor is shut down by inserting the control rods fully into the core of the reactor (see p. 68). When this occurs, less than one neutron per fission on average is available for further fission so the rate of fission reactions decreases.
- An **atomic bomb** is designed so that more than one neutron per fission on average goes on to produce further fission. As a result, a huge amount of energy is released in a very short time.

### Note

**'Fission' means the nucleus splits into two fragments**

# The thermal nuclear reactor

- The fuel is **enriched uranium** which is mostly U-238 (which absorbs neutrons without fission) and 2–3% U-235; the fuel is contained in sealed hollow metal tubes; neutrons pass through the tube walls. The fuel rods become very hot in the reactor.
- The fuel rods are in a **moderator** (e.g. a graphite core). The fission neutrons repeatedly collide with moderator atoms and are slowed down enough to cause further fission when they re-enter the fuel rods.
- A **coolant** fluid (e.g. carbon dioxide gas) is pumped through channels in the core to remove thermal energy from the core. The hot coolant is used to generate steam in a **heat exchanger**. The steam is used to drive turbines coupled to **a.c. generators**.
- **Control rods** of boron or cadmium are inserted into the core to maintain a steady chain reaction. The control rods absorb surplus neutrons to ensure exactly one neutron per fission goes on to produce further fission.
- After use, the fuel rods and **spent fuel** are highly radioactive. The rods are stored in cooling ponds then reprocessed to recover unused fuel. The waste products are stored underground in sealed containers. Low level waste (e.g. air filters, clothing) and intermediate level waste (e.g. chemicals used for reprocessing) are also stored in sealed containers.

## Key words to remember

fission; the splitting of a U-235 nucleus in two fragments

U–235; an isotope of uranium

control rods; used to maintain a steady rate of production of energy

moderator; used to slow down fast neutrons

coolant; used to take thermal energy away from the reactor core

heat exchanger; used to transfer thermal energy from the coolant to raise steam

# Inside a nuclear reactor

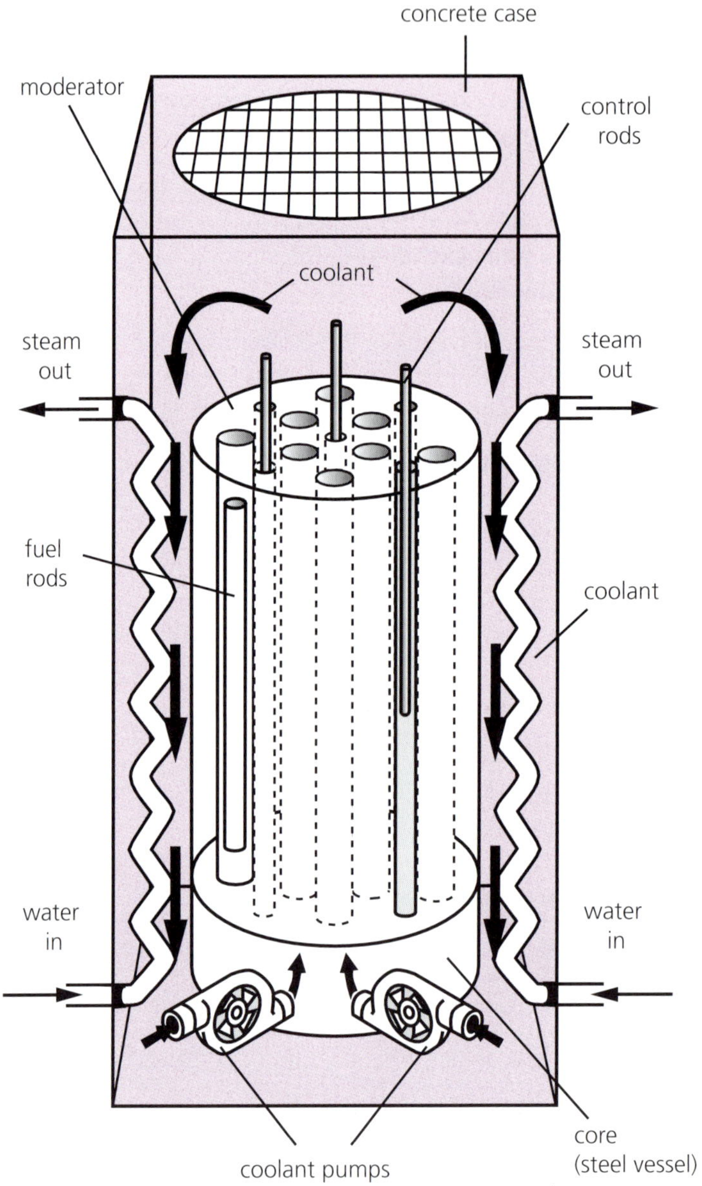

# Radioactivity quiz

## Questions

**1** How many protons and how many neutrons are present in a $^{238}_{92}U$ nucleus?

**2** How many protons and how many neutrons are present in a particle?

**3** Which type of radiation from a radioactive substance is capable of penetrating a £1 coin?

**4** Which type of radiation from a radioactive isotope has a range in air of no more than about 100 mm?

**5** State one cause of background radioactivity.

**6** Define the activity of a radioactive isotope and state the unit of activity.

**7** The activity of a radioactive isotope decreases from 8 MBq to 2 MBq in 12 hours. What is the half-life of this radioactive isotope?

**8** What type of radiation is used to kill bacteria in foods?

**9** Which type of particle causes nuclear fission in a nuclear reactor?

**10** What is the purpose of the control rods in a nuclear reactor?

**Answers**

**1** 92 protons and 146 neutrons **2** 2 protons and 2 neutrons **3** g radiation **4** a radiation **5** Radioactive isotopes in rocks or cosmic radiation from space or radiation from the Sun **6** The number of disintegrations per second; the becquerel **7** 6 hours **8** g radiation **9** The neutron **10** To absorb surplus neutrons to ensure exactly one neutron per fission goes on to produce further fission

# Electricity 5

## Electric charge

- **Electrons** are tiny negatively charged particles contained in every atom. The nucleus of every atom is composed of protons and neutrons. Protons are positively charged particles.
- Neutrons are uncharged.
- An **uncharged object** contains equal numbers of protons and electrons.
- An **insulator** contains electrons that are firmly held to individual atoms.
- A **conductor** contains electrons that move about freely inside the conductor.

## Charging

- Some insulators can be charged by friction. This process causes transfer of electrons to or from the insulator. Insulators that gain electrons become negative, insulators that lose electrons become positive.
- Any insulated conductor can be charged negatively by gaining electrons or positively by losing electrons.

### The law of force between charged objects

Objects that carry the same type of charge repel each other: a positively charged object and a negatively charged object attract each other.

**Like charges repel : unlike charges attract**.

#### A paper puzzle

Rub a Perspex ruler with a dry cloth and you will find the ruler can pick up uncharged bits of paper. This happens because paper is not a perfect insulator. The positively charged Perspex rod attracts electrons to the nearest side of the paper, leaving the far side of the paper positive. The force of attraction on the near side is greater than the force of repulsion on the far side of the paper. The bit of paper is therefore held on the rod.

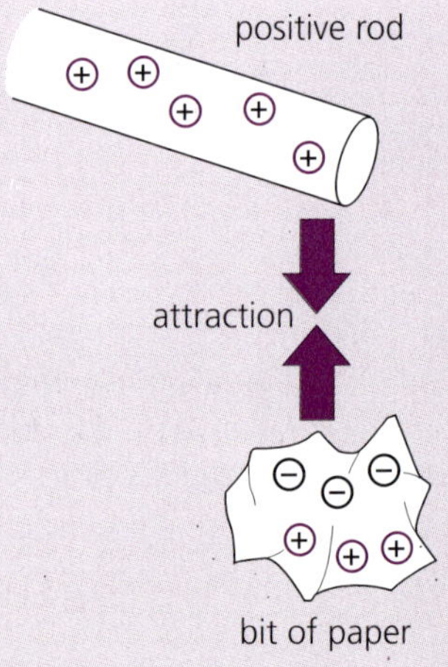

# The gold leaf electroscope

This device is used to find out if an object is charged and whether the charge is a negative or positive charge.

- If a **negatively charged object** is touched on the cap of an uncharged electroscope the electroscope leaf rises because the electroscope gains electrons from the object. The leaf and stem of the electroscope both become charged negatively so they repel each other.
- If a **positively charged object** is touched on the cap of an uncharged electroscope, the electroscope leaf rises because the leaf and stem of the electroscope both become charged positively and repel each other.
- To **find out if a charged object carries positive or negative charge** the electroscope is charged with a known type of charge so its leaf rises. If the charged object to be investigated is then brought near the cap of the electroscope the leaf rises if the object is charged the same as the electroscope.

## Detecting negative charge

negative rod brought near negatively charged electroscope

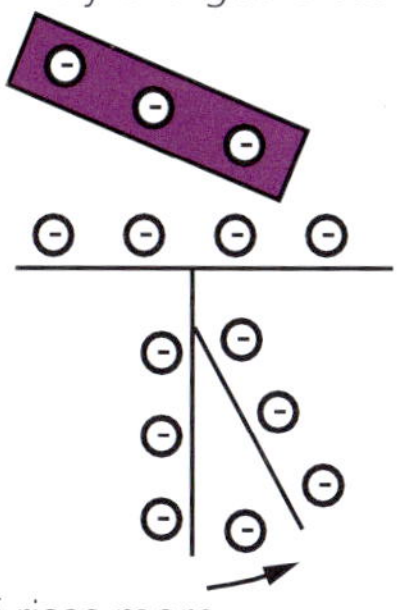

leaf rises more

## Detecting positive charge

positive rod brought near positively charged electroscope

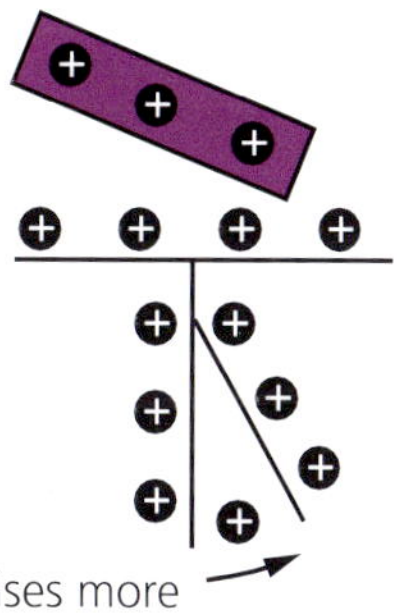

leaf rises more

Remember

A metal contains free electrons that move about in the metal. An insulated metal is made positive by removing free electrons from it.

# Electrostatics at work

## Earthing

A **charged metal object** loses its charge if it is 'earthed'. If the object is initially positive, it attracts electrons from the ground to become uncharged. If the object is initially negative, it loses electrons to the ground to become uncharged.

### Electrostatics applications include:

- the capacitor, used to store charge
- the electrostatic paint spray, used to spray a fine mist of paint droplets evenly onto a metal surface
- the electrostatic precipitator, used to prevent dust particles produced in coal-burning power stations escaping into the atmosphere

The ash and dust from coal burned at a power station is prevented from entering the atmosphere by an electrostatic precipitator in the chimney. The dust particles touch the charged wire grid of the precipitator and become charged. The particles are then attracted on to the earthed metal tube surrounding the grid.

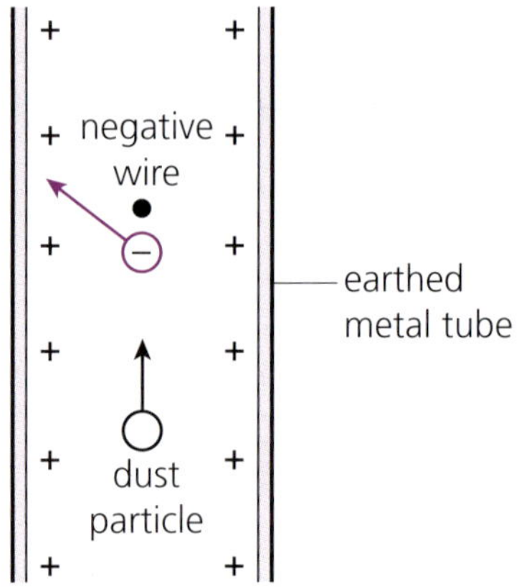


Attracting dust particles

- the photocopier, used to make the toner powder stick on the image
- the digital camera
- the lightning conductor, used to protect buildings from thunderbolts.

### Electrostatic hazards

- Explosion risk due to sparks (e.g. when powders or flammable liquids flow through pipes or in an operating theatre where flammable vapours may be present).
- High voltage shock to the human body.
- Damage to computer chips.

Charge on an insulated conductor is most concentrated at sharp points – if the conductor is in air, charge may leak off at these points due to ionisation.

# Charge and current

An electric current is a flow of charge carried by charged particles. Electrons carry charge through a metal. Ions carry charge through an electrolyte. Metal ions always carry a positive charge.

For a constant current,

| **Charge** | = | **current** | x | **time**. |
|---|---|---|---|---|
| (in coulombs) | | (in amperes) | | (in seconds) |

## Electrolysis

**Electrolytic conduction** occurs when a compound (molten or in solution) conducts electricity. In the process the compound is decomposed (i.e. broken down into simpler substances). In an electrolytic cell, the **electrolyte** is the conducting liquid, the **anode** is the positive electrode and the **cathode** is the negative electrode.

## Copper-plating a key

Each copper ion in solution is short of two electrons and therefore carries a fixed positive charge. The copper ions are attracted to the metal cathode.

To keep the concentration of copper ions in the solution constant, the anode also needs to be copper. Copper atoms from the anode give up electrons and go into the solution as copper ions.

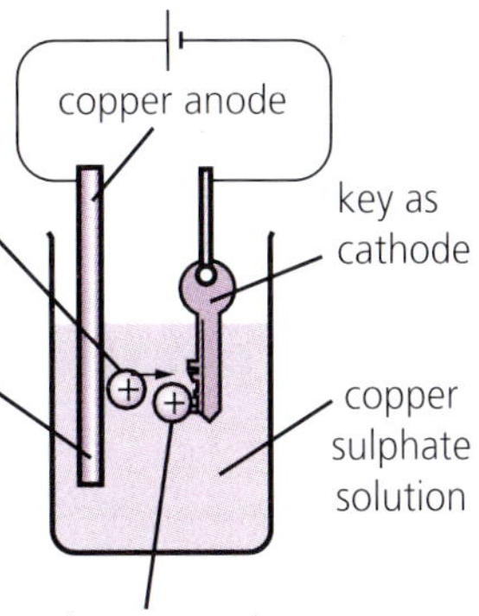


At the cathode each copper ion gains two electrons to become an uncharged atom. The copper atom sticks to the metal cathode. A layer of copper is formed on the cathode.

The mass of copper deposited on the cathode is in proportion to the charge passed.

# Current and potential difference

- **Potential difference** (in volts) between two points in a circuit

$$= \frac{\text{electrical energy delivered (in joules)}}{\text{charge supplied (in coulombs)}}$$

- **Resistance** in ohms (Ω) $= \dfrac{\text{potential difference (in volts)}}{\text{current (in amperes)}}$

## Components in series

- The same current passes through each component.
- The total p.d. = the sum of the p.d.s across the components.
- For two resistors $R_1$ and $R_2$ in series, the total resistance = $R_1 + R_2$.

## Serial resistors

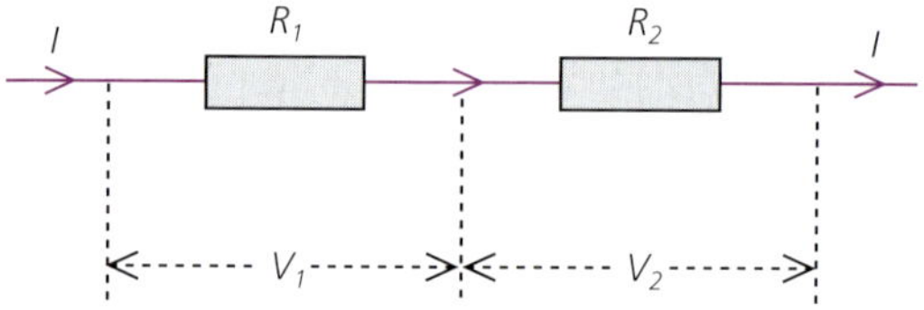


## Components in parallel

- Components in parallel have the same potential difference.
- The total current = the sum of the currents through the components.
- At a junction, the total current in = the total current out.

## Parallel resistors

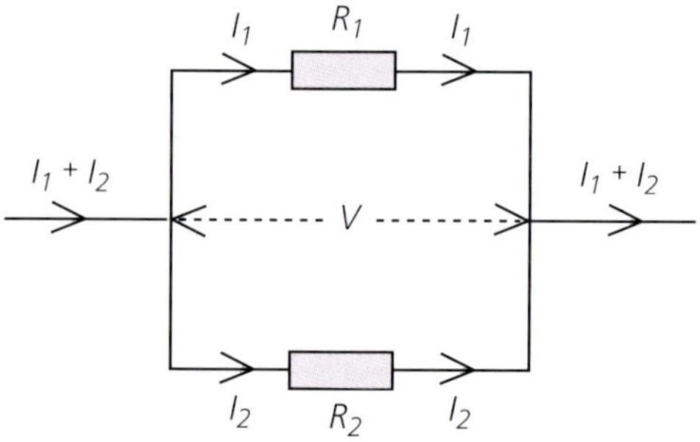

# More on resistance

## Measurement of the resistance of a resistor

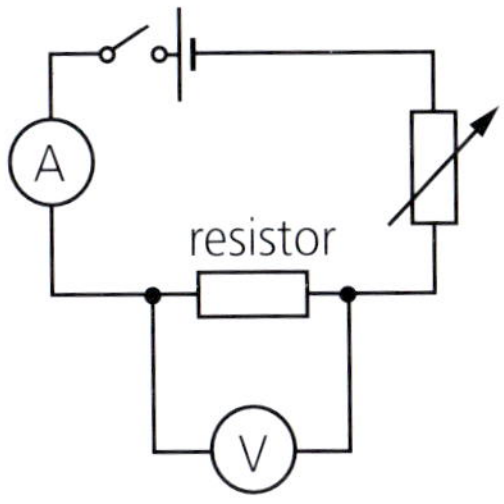


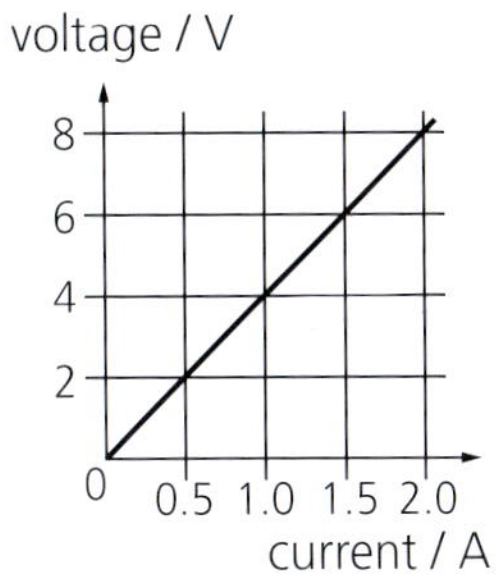


Use the **variable resistor** to alter the current. Measure the current from the ammeter and the p.d. from the voltmeter. Plot a graph of p.d. against current to give a straight line through the origin. The resistance is the gradient of the line.

## Heating effect

Heat is dissipated in a resistor when a current is passed through it.

**Electrical power supplied**
= **current** x **potential difference** = **current**$^2$ x **resistance**.

The p.d. is the energy delivered to the resistor when 1 coulomb of charge passes through it.

The current is the number of coulombs of charge that pass through the resistor each second.

Therefore the energy delivered per second = energy delivered per coulomb x no. of coulombs passing through per second = p.d. x current.

### Question

What is the resistance of the resistor in the circuit above?

**Answer**

4Ω $\left(= \frac{8V}{2A}\right)$

# Component characteristics

A component is any object connected into a circuit. The circuit on p. 75 may be used to investigate the current through a component for different p.d.s across it. The result may be plotted as a graph of current (on the y-axis) versus p.d. (on the x-axis).

- A **resistor** gives a straight line through 0. The greater the resistance, the less steep the line is.
- A **filament bulb** gives a curve through 0. The curve becomes less steep as the current increases because the resistance becomes greater as the filament becomes hotter.

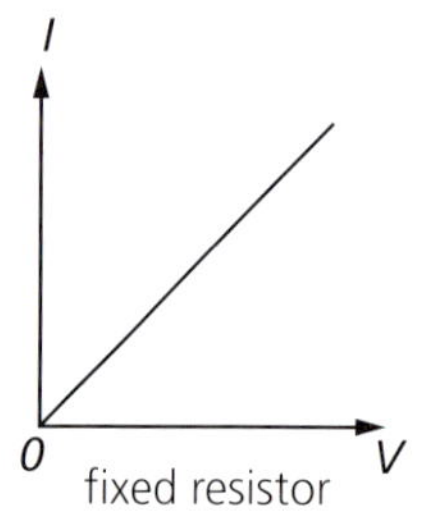


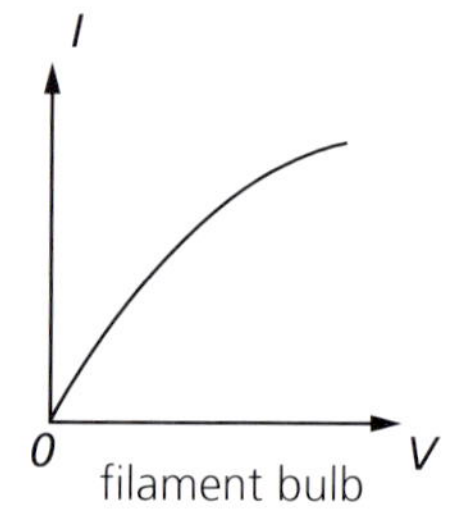


- A **light-dependent resistor** (**LDR**) under constant illumination gives a straight line through 0, indicating its resistance is constant. The higher the light intensity on it, the lower the resistance of the LDR.
- A **thermistor** at constant temperature also gives a straight line. The higher the temperature, the lower the resistance of the thermistor.
- A **diode** conducts in one direction only (the forward direction) provided the p.d. exceeds about 0.6 V.

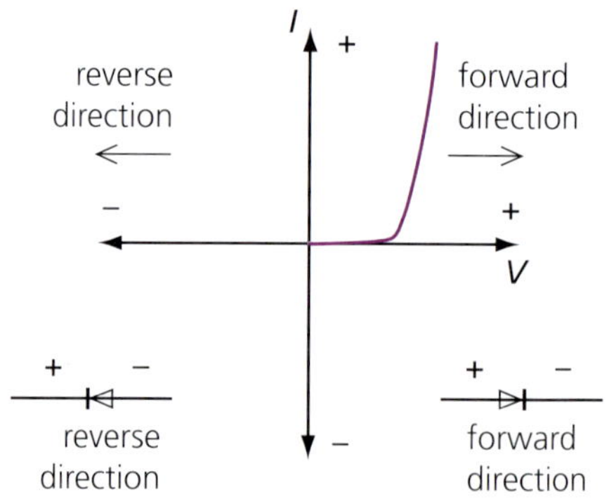

# Component symbols

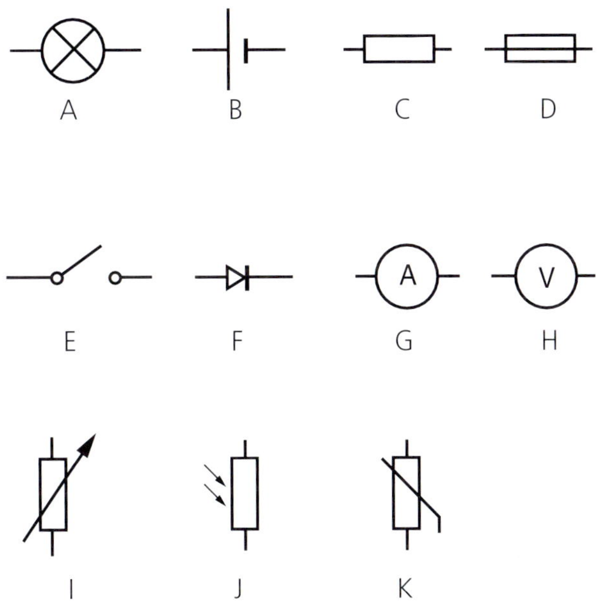


A light bulb

B cell

C resistor

D fuse

E switch

F diode

G ammeter

H voltmeter

I variable resistor

J light dependent resistor

K thermistor

# Mains electricity

In Britain, mains electricity is alternating current at 50 Hz. Mains electricity is supplied via a **live** conductor and a **neutral** conductor which is earthed at the local sub-station.

## Alternating current

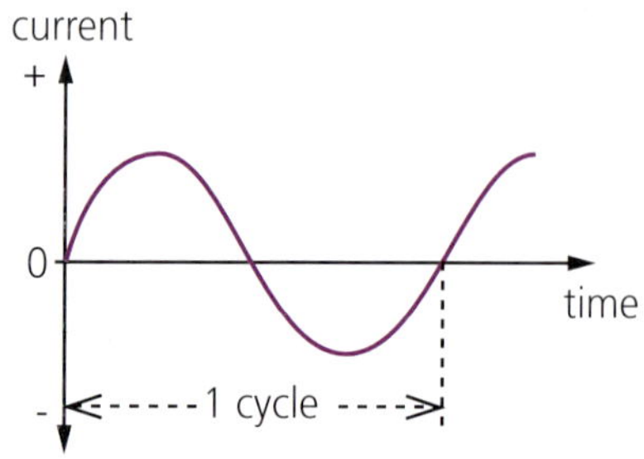


The **ring main** (see p. 79) includes an earth wire that is connected to earth at the premises. A **three-pin plug** (see p. 80) is used to connect an appliance to the ring main.

If the appliance has a metal frame, the frame must be **earthed** via the three-pin plug. This is to protect the user in case a live wire touches the frame (see p.80). Lighting circuits do not usually include an earth wire.

**Fuses and circuit breakers** (see p. 81) are designed to cut the current off in the live wire if the current exceeds the rated value of the fuse or circuit breaker. They are designed to prevent excessive current which would cause overheating.

## Double insulation

Mains appliances with insulated cases are double-insulated for safety.

### Symbol

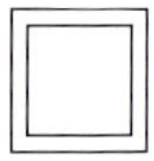

# Mains circuits

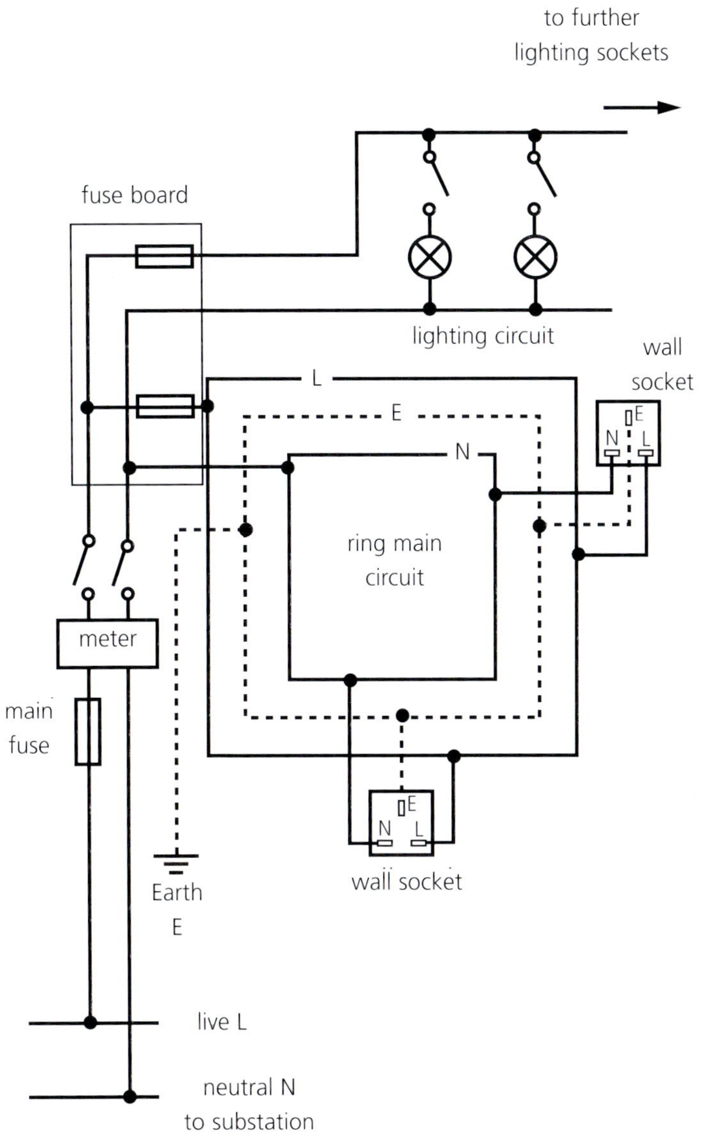

# Earthing

## The three-pin plug

The metal case of a mains appliance is connected to earth via the three-pin plug.

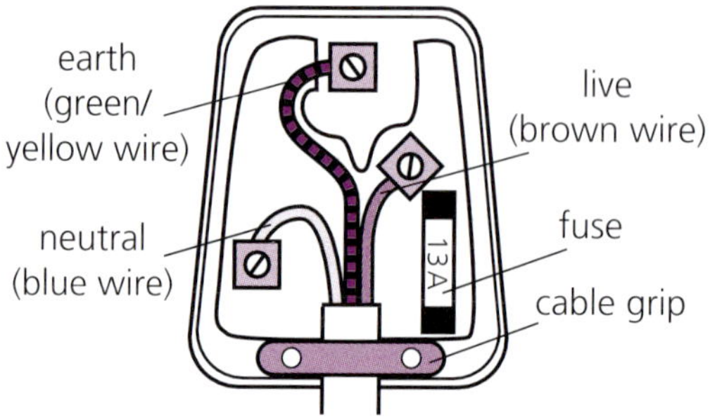


### Mains electricity is lethal

The human body conducts electricity. If the metal case of a mains appliance should become **live** (perhaps as a result of a live wire breaking off a terminal and making contact with the case) anyone touching the case would be electrocuted if the case was not earthed. This would happen because electricity would pass between the case and the ground via the body.

### Earthing protects the user not the appliance

An appliance with an earthed case might develop a fault which causes current to pass through the live wire and the case to earth instead of through the live and neutral wires. This current might not be sufficient to trip a circuit breaker or melt a fuse wire. However, it might be enough to cause the appliance to over heat. Also, if the earth wire connection to the case were to break, the case would then become live and therefore lethal.

# Fuses and circuit breakers

Faulty insulation can cause a **short-circuit** which is a low-resistance path between two points in a circuit. If this occurs, the current through the wires increases which may cause the wires to overheat.

## Circuit breaker

This 'trips' if too much current passes through it. A circuit breaker is a switch in the live wire that opens if the current in the live wire becomes too large. The switch stays open after it is opened and is reset manually. Before it is reset, the fault causing the excess current must be remedied. In a **residual current circuit breaker**, switches in the live wire and the neutral wire are both opened if the current in the neutral wire is **different** to the current in the live wire.

## Fuse

This contains a thin wire that melts if too much current passes through the fuse. A fuse in an appliance or in a three-pin plug connected to an appliance is designed to melt if the current exceeds the current rating of the appliance. This can be calculated using the electrical power equation (see p. 75) if the power rating of the appliance and the mains voltage are known. The fuse rating should be a little higher than the current rating of the appliance.

For example, a 3 kW, 240 V electric heater should be fitted with a 13 A fuse. The current rating of the heater is 12.5 A (= 3000 W/240 V)

### Note

Electrical faults can cause short-circuits. A short-circuit occurs where a fault creates a low-resistance path between the live wire and the neutral wire or earth.

A fuse or a circuit breaker is designed to prevent excessive current which would overheat the wires. Before a blown fuse is replaced or a circuit breaker is reset, the fault must be corrected.

A residual current circuit breaker protects the user as it is activated if the live current and the neutral current differ by a tiny amount.

# Electricity costs

An electricity meter is fitted in every home or shop or office to measure the electrical energy supplied to the premises. The meter is usually read every three months and an electricity bill is supplied giving the cost of the electrical energy supplied since the last time the meter was read. Electricity meters record electricity usage in **kilowatt hours**, usually simply referred to as 'units' of electricity.

- One **kilowatt hour** (**kWh**) is the electrical energy supplied to a one kilowatt appliance in one hour. Since 1 kilowatt equals 1000 watts which is 1000 joules per second and 1 hour = 3600 seconds, then
  1 kilowatt hour = 3.6 MJ (= 1000 x 3600 J).
- The **unit cost of electricity** is the cost per kilowatt hour of electrical energy. If an electricity company charges 6p per unit, the cost of 2000 units of electricity from this company would therefore be £120 (= 2000 x 6p).
- The **number of units** used by an appliance in a given time can be worked out if its power rating is known. For example, a 3.0 kW electric heater used for 2 hours would use 6 units (= 3.0 kW x 2 hours) of electricity.
- The **total number of units** used by a collection of appliances in a certain period can be worked out if the power rating and the time of usage of each appliance is known.

*Example*

a 3.0 kW heater used for 2 hours = 3.0 kW x 2 hours = 6 units;
a 7.0 kW shower used for 0.5 hours = 7.0 kW x 0.5 hours = 3.5 units;
the total number of units used = 6 + 3.5 = 9.5 units.

The total cost at 6p per unit = 9.5 x 6 = 57p.

## Quick Quiz

1. Calculate the number of units of electricity used when:
   (a) a 3 kW heater is used for 2 hours
   (b) a 0.5 kW hairdrier is used for 30 minutes
   (c) a 100 W lightbulb is used for 24 hours
   (d) a 6 kW electric shower is used for 20 minutes.
2. A 200 W spot light is designed to last for 1000 hours.
   (a) How many units of electricity would it use?
   (b) Calculate the total cost of the units in (a) if the cost per unit is 5p.

**Answers**
1. (a) 6 (b) 0.25
   (c) 2.4 (d) 2
2. (a) 200 (b) £10

# Electricity quiz

## Questions

**1** A plastic ruler is charged positively by rubbing it with a dry cloth. In terms of electrons, explain what happens in this process.

**2** A gold leaf electroscope is charged negatively. The leaf of the electroscope rises when a charged object is held near the electroscope cap. What type of charge does the object carry?

**3** When an insulated charged metal object was earthed, electrons transferred from the Earth to the object. What type of charge did the object possess before it was earthed?

**4** Calculate the time taken for 3 coulombs to pass through a component in a circuit when the current through the component is 0.2 A.

**5** Calculate the energy delivered in 1 minute to a 0.5 Ω resistor when a steady current of 2 A passes through it.

**6** How does the resistance of a filament torch bulb change as the current is increased through it?

**7** How does the resistance of a thermistor change as its temperature falls?

**8** What is the purpose of a fuse in an electrical circuit?

**9** What current passes through the filament of a 150 W, 240 V light bulb when it is switched on?

**10** Why is it important that any mains appliance with a metal case should be earthed?

**Answers**

**1** Electrons transfer from the ruler to the cloth **2** Negative **3** Positive **4** 15 s **5** 120 J **6** Increases **7** Increases **8** To switch the circuit off if the current exceeds a certain value **9** 0.63 A **10** To prevent the case from becoming live. If this happened, anyone touching it would receive an electric shock which might be fatal

# Electromagnetism 6

## Magnetic fields

### Permanent magnets

**like poles repel : unlike poles attract**

A freely-pivoted bar magnet lines up with one end pointing north (the north-seeking end) and the other end pointing south. The lines of force of a bar magnet are given by the direction which a plotting compass points along. The lines loop round from its north pole to its south pole. Permanent magnets are made from steel not iron because steel retains its magnetism better.

### Magnetic fields

bar magnet

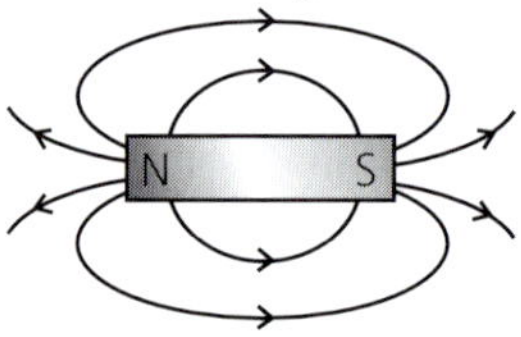


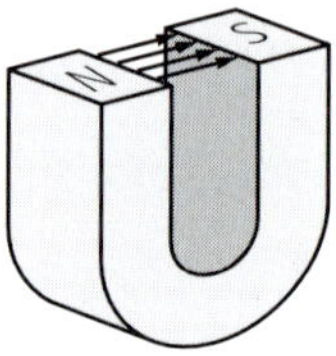


U-shaped magnet

## The magnetic effect on an electric current

- **Near a long straight wire** the lines of force are concentric circles centred on the wire in a plane perpendicular to the wire.
- **Near a solenoid** (i.e. a long coil) the lines of force pass through the solenoid along its axis and loop round outside the solenoid from one end to the other end like a bar magnet.
- The strength of the magnetic field due to a current-carrying wire at a given position increases with the current.

# Electromagnets

An electromagnet consists of a solenoid with an iron core. The iron core becomes strongly magnetised when the current is switched on and loses its magnetism when the current is switched off. Electromagnets are made from iron not steel because iron loses its magnetism more easily.

## Uses of an electromagnet

**In a scrap yard crane** a strong electromagnet is attached to the end of the crane cable. The electromagnet attracts iron and steel objects when it is switched on. Ferrous objects such as car bodies can be moved about in this way. When the current is switched off, the ferrous object held by the electromagnet falls off.

**An electric bell or a buzzer** consists of an electromagnet and a **make-and-break** switch. When a battery is connected across the bell terminals, the electromagnet is magnetised and attracts the iron armature. The hammer hits the bell as a result. The movement of the armature opens the make-and-break switch which switches the current off. The electromagnet loses its magnetism and releases the armature to close the make-and-break switch again. This cycle happens repeatedly making the bell ring continuously.

## An electric bell

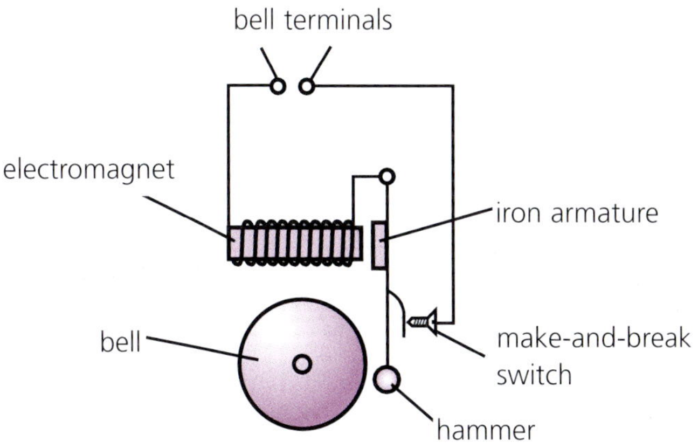

# More uses of electromagnets

The **relay coil** is used to open a switch which is in a separate circuit. Usually the switch is used to switch on and off a much larger current than the current through the relay coil. When a current is passed through the relay coil, the electromagnet becomes magnetised and attracts the iron armature. The movement of the armature opens or closes a switch which is in a different circuit.

## A normally-open relay

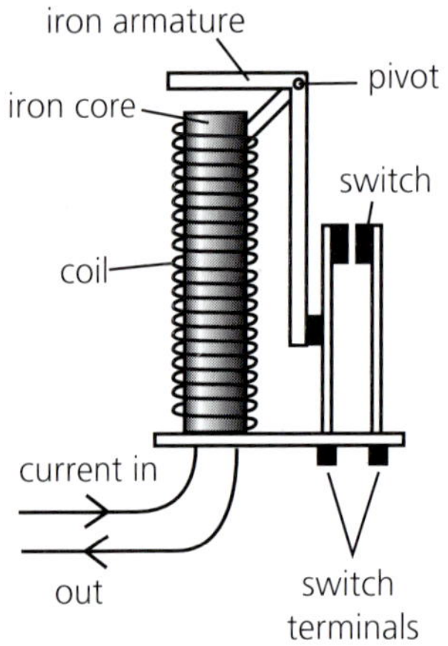


**Normally-open** relays are designed so the switch closes when current passes through the relay coil.

**Normally-closed** relays are designed so the switch opens when current is passed through the relay coil.

The **recorder head of a tape recorder** is a small U-shaped electromagnet which presses against a magnetic tape. The electromagnet is supplied with the audio signal which is recorded on the tape in the form of varying magnetism along its length as the tape winds past. To play the signal back, the tape is played back and the electromagnet is used to generate an alternating voltage from the variations of the tape's magnetism. (See p. 91.)

## Quick quiz

Fill in the missing words from the following list.
*armature iron switch*
A relay coil consists of an electromagnet and a switch. The electromagnet has an __________ core. When current passes through the coil of the electromagnet, the __________ is attracted to the iron core.
In a normally-open relay, the movement of the armature causes the __________ gap to close.

**Answers**
iron, armature,
switch

# The motor effect

- When a current-carrying wire is at a non-zero angle to the lines of force of a magnetic field, a force acts on the wire at right angles to the wire and to the lines of force.

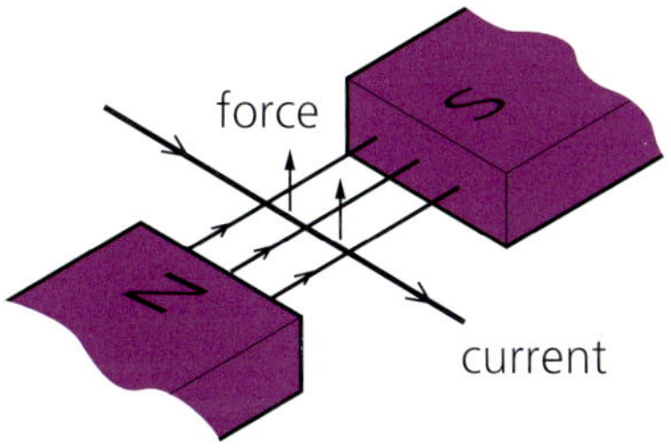


- The left-hand rule (First finger Field; seCond finger Current; thuMb Motion) gives the direction of the force if the direction of the current and the lines of force are known.

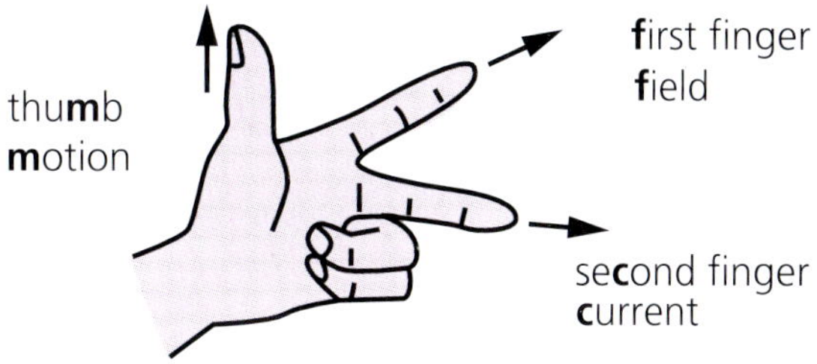


The **loudspeaker** (where the current is alternating); the force on the coil wire alternates in direction because the current alternates. The coil therefore vibrates at the same frequency as the alternating current. This makes the diaphragm vibrate to create sound waves in the surrounding air.

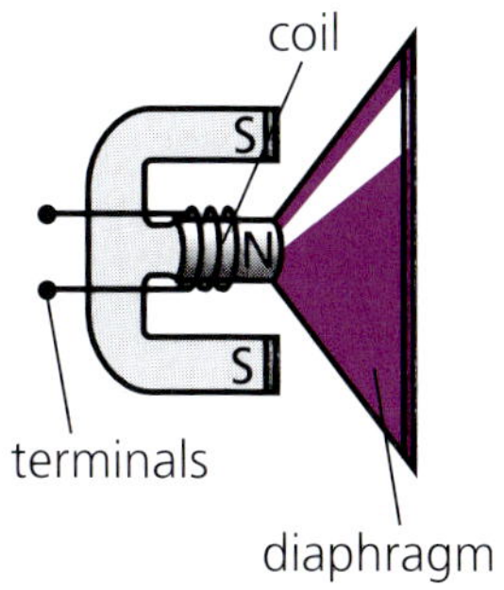

# The d.c. electric motor

When the coil is in the same plane as the lines of force, each long side is acted on by a force which causes the coil to spin. When the coil is perpendicular to the lines of force, the **split-ring commutator** reverses the direction of current round the coil so it is forced to keep rotating in the same direction.

Current passes along each side of the coil in opposite directions. Each side is therefore acted on by a force due to the magnetic field. The force on one side is in the opposite direction to the force on the other side.

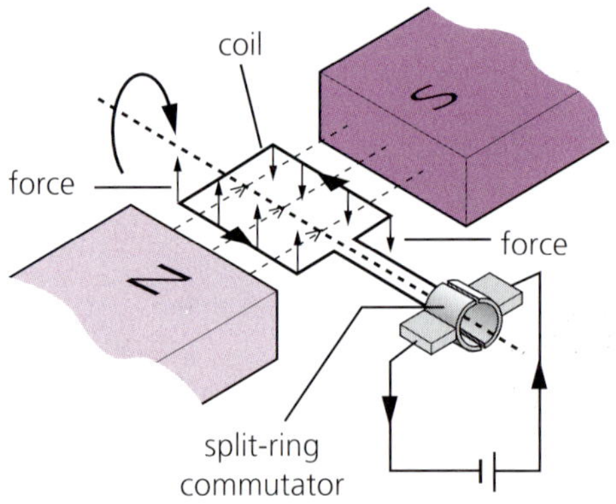


When the coil is parallel to the field, the forces on the sides rotate the coil. As the coil turns through the position at 90° to the field, the split-ring commutator reverses its connections to the battery, reversing the current direction round the coil.

Rotation by more than 90° has swapped the positions of the two sides **and** reversed the current direction in the coil. Therefore, the forces acting on each side continue to turn the coil in the same direction as before, so the coil rotates continuously in one direction.

# Electromagnetic induction

- When a wire cuts across the lines of force of a magnetic field, a voltage is induced in the wire. The faster the wire cuts across the field lines, the greater the induced voltage.
- If the wire is part of a complete circuit, the induced voltage makes a current pass round the circuit. The direction of the induced current is always such as to oppose the change that causes it.
- If the wire is moved along the direction of the lines of force so it does not cut the lines no voltage is induced.

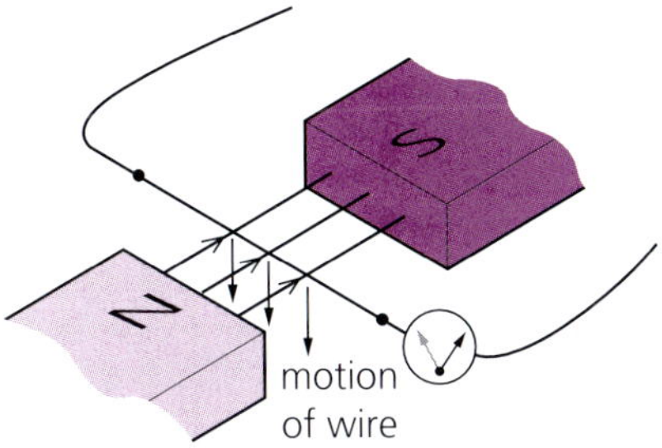


## Laws of electromagnetic induction

- **Faraday's law** states that the induced voltage is proportional to the speed at which the wire cuts the lines of force.
- **Lenz's law** states that the induced current always acts in such a direction as to oppose the change that causes it – for example, if the north pole of a bar magnet is pushed into a coil connected to a meter, the induced current creates a magnetic field that opposes the incoming north pole.

### Note

To generate a voltage, the wire must **cut** across the lines of force of the magnetic field.

# The alternating current generator

This consists of a coil forced to spin in a magnetic field. An **alternating voltage** is induced in the coil which is connected to an external circuit via two slip rings. Alternating current therefore passes round the coil and the external circuit. A split-ring commutator instead of two slip rings would give full-wave direct current.

- The induced voltage is at a maximum (+ or –) when the coil is parallel to the lines of force of the field. The sides of the coil cut directly across the lines of force in this position.
- The induced voltage is zero when the coil is perpendicular to the lines of force of the field. The sides of the coil do not cut the lines of force at this position.
- The faster the coil spins, the higher the **peak value** and the **frequency** of the alternating voltage.

Note

**Voltage** means electrical energy transferred per unit charge regardless of whether or not electrical energy is being used or being generated.

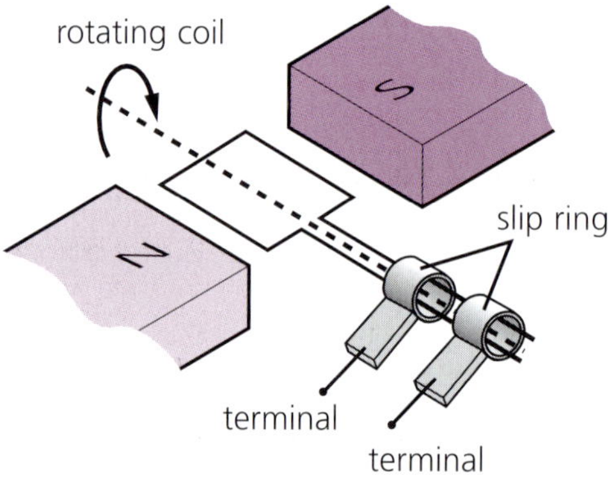


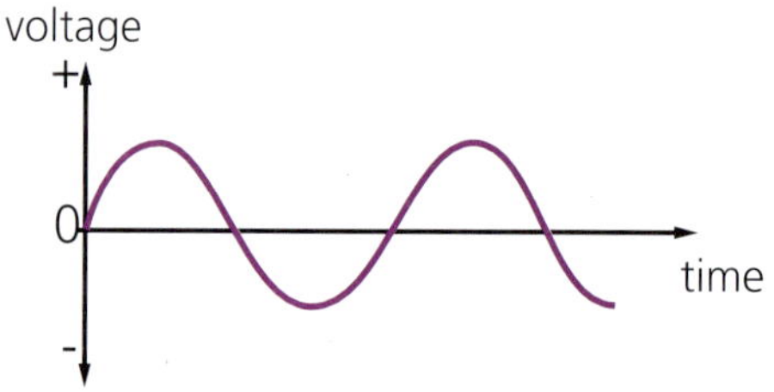

# More applications of electromagnetic induction

## The dynamo

The magnet is forced to rotate in a U-shaped iron core which a coil is wrapped around. The rotating magnet induces a voltage in the coil. The faster the magnet rotates, the larger the voltage.

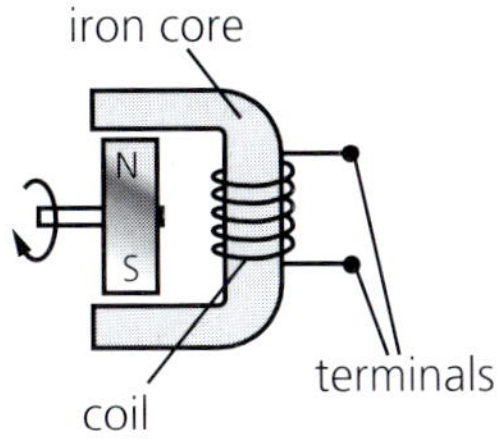


## The microphone

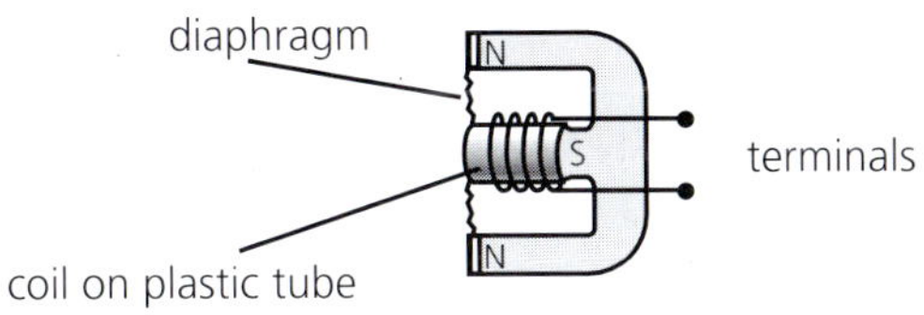


Sound waves make the diaphragm vibrate. The coil attached to the diaphragm therefore vibrates. Since the coil is in a magnetic field, an alternating voltage is induced in the coil.

## A tape recorder on 'playback'

The tape is moved past the recording head which is a small electromagnet. The varying magnetism of the tape induces a voltage in the coil of the electromagnet. This induced voltage is the same as the audio signal which was recorded on the tape (see p. 86).

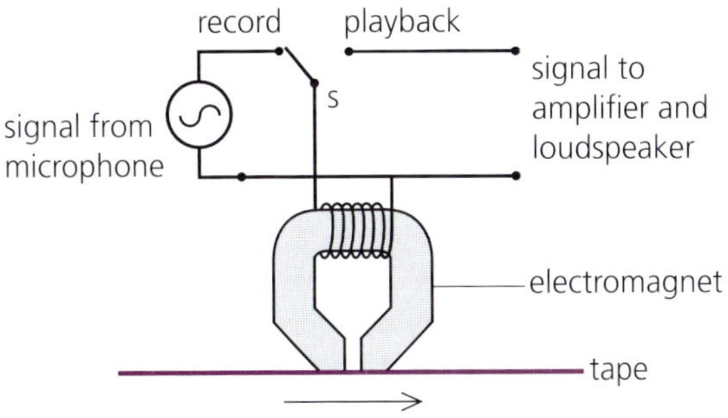

# The transformer

A transformer consists of two insulated coils of wire (the **primary** and the **secondary** coils) wound on the same iron core. When alternating current is passed through the primary coil, a changing magnetic field is set up in the core. This changing magnetic field induces an **alternating voltage** in the secondary coil.

A transformer is designed to **change the peak value of an alternating voltage**, either stepping it up or stepping it down.

$$\frac{\text{Voltage induced in the secondary coil}}{\text{Voltage applied to the primary coil}} = \frac{\text{Number of turns on the secondary coil}}{\text{Number of turns in the primary coil}}$$

For 100% efficiency:

secondary current x secondary voltage = primary current x primary voltage.

Practical transformers are very efficient. The causes of inefficiency of a transformer are due to:

- resistance heating of the coil wires
- energy used to magnetise and demagnetise the core repeatedly
- induced currents in the core itself. These are referred to as 'eddy' currents.

Electric power is transmitted on the Grid System at high voltage and low current to reduce power loss due to resistance heating of the cables.

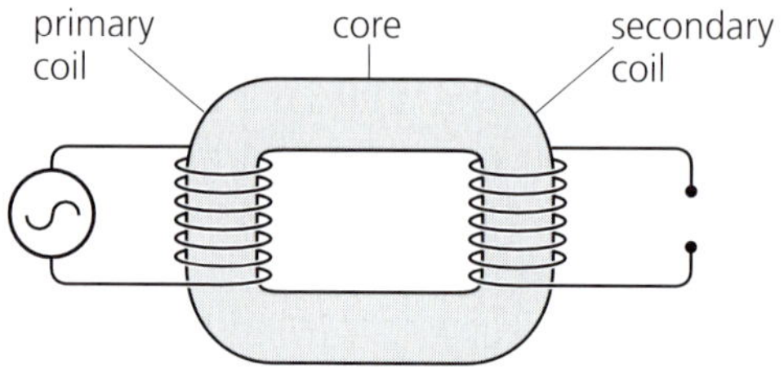


transformer symbol

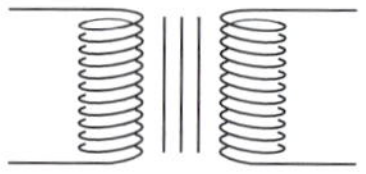

**Note**

The voltage ratio is equal to the turns ratio. A step-up transformer has more secondary turns than primary turns. A step-down transformer has fewer secondary turns than primary turns.

# Electromagnetism quiz

## Questions

1 End X of a bar magnet was held near a plotting compass attracting the tail of the compass needle. What was the polarity of end X?

2 Why is the core of an electromagnet made from iron not steel.

3 Why is a permanent magnet made from steel not iron?

4 Why is the armature of an electric bell not made of steel?

5 What is the advantage of a circuit breaker in comparison with a fuse?

6 What is the purpose of a split-ring commutator in an electric motor?

7 What is the angle between the coil of a simple a.c. generator and the lines of force of the magnetic field when the induced voltage is zero?

8 Outline how a microphone works.

9 A transformer is to be used to step up an alternating voltage from 12 V to 240 V. The primary coil has 100 turns. How many turns should the secondary coil have?

10 Why is electrical power transmitted through the grid system at high voltage?

**Answers**

**1** North **2** Iron loses its magnetism easily when the current is switched off **3** Steel retains its magnetism better than iron **4** It would be magnetised by the electromagnet and would stick to it when the electromagnet is switched off **5** A circuit breaker does not need to be replaced each time it switches the current off **6** To reverse the current in the coil each time the coil is perpendicular to the lines of force **7** 90° **8** Sound waves make a diaphragm vibrate. A coil attached to the diaphragm vibrates in a magnetic field. This movement induces an alternating voltage in the coil **9** 2000 **10** The higher the voltage, the smaller the current for the same power. The smaller the current the less the power wasted due to resistance heating of the cables

# Sample Mind Maps

## Electricity – Mind Map

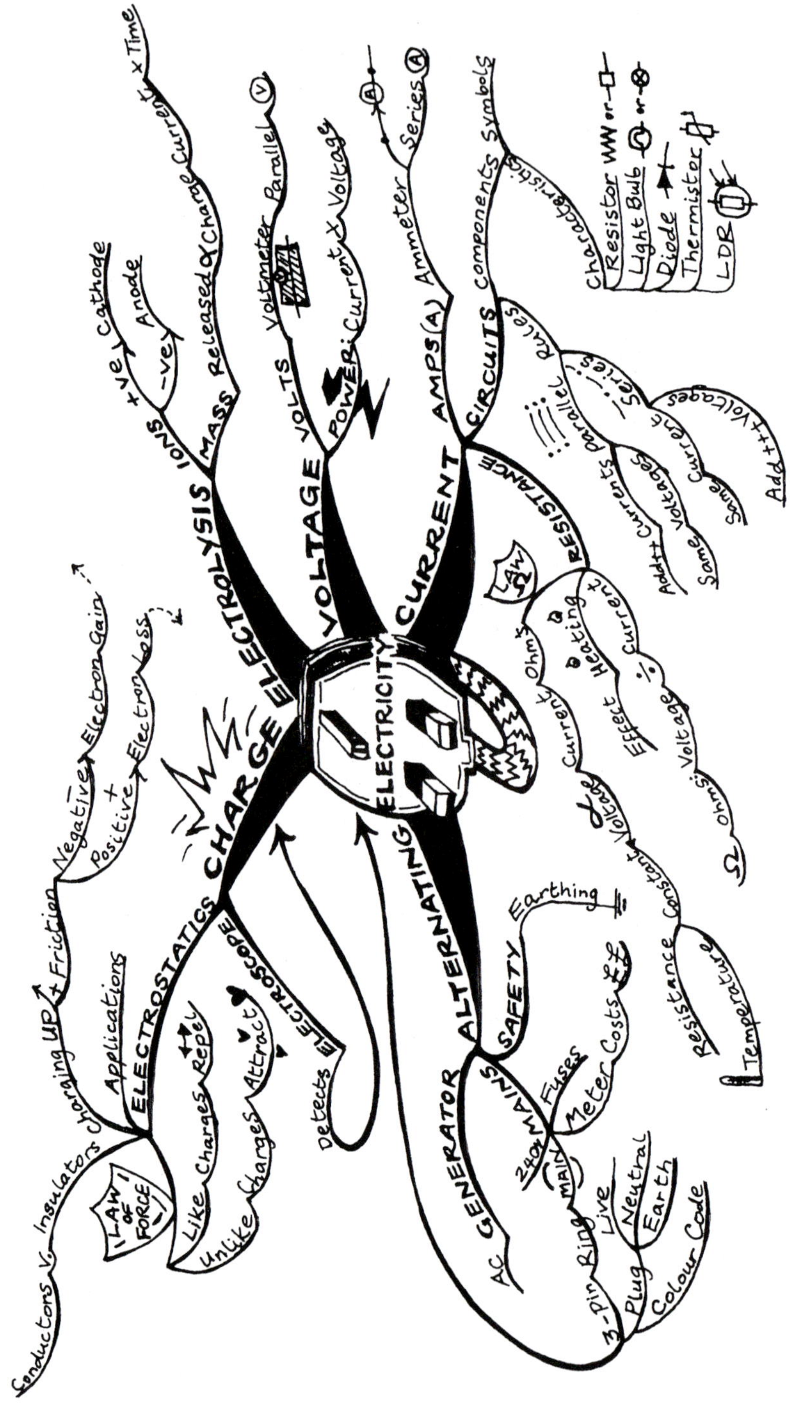

## Electromagnetism – Mind Map

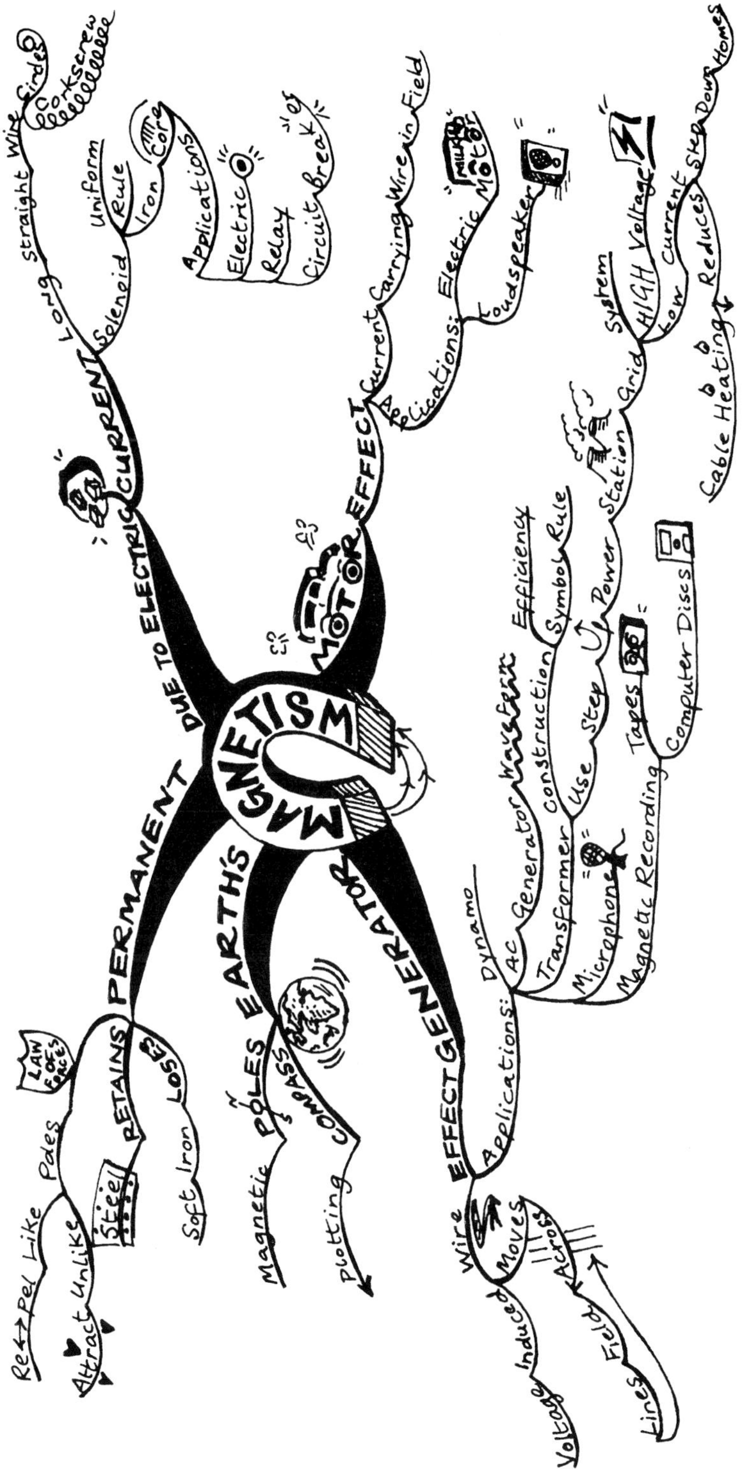

# Equations you should know

Read, learn and inwardly digest the formulas and units below. To test yourself, cover each line with a blank card after the first word and see if you can write the rest of the equation on the card.

$$\text{voltage} = \text{current} \times \text{resistance}$$

$$\underset{(\text{J})}{\text{energy transferred}} = \underset{(\text{W})}{\text{power}} \times \underset{(\text{s})}{\text{time}}$$

$$\underset{(\text{kWh})}{\text{energy transferred}} = \underset{(\text{kW})}{\text{power}} \times \underset{(\text{h})}{\text{time}}$$

$$\text{pressure} = \frac{\text{force}}{\text{area}}$$

$$\text{speed} = \frac{\text{distance}}{\text{time}}$$

$$\text{work done} = \text{force} \times \text{distance moved in direction of force}$$

$$\text{energy transferred} = \text{work done}$$

$$\text{efficiency} = \frac{\text{useful energy transferred by device}}{\text{total energy supplied to device}}$$

$$\text{power} = \frac{\text{work done}}{\text{time taken}}$$

$$\text{weight} = \text{mass} \times \text{gravitational field strength } (g)$$

$$\text{charge} = \text{current} \times \text{time}$$

$$\text{energy transferred} = \text{potential difference} \times \text{charge}$$

$$\frac{\text{voltage across coil 1}}{\text{voltage across coil 2}} = \frac{\text{number of turns in coil 1}}{\text{number of turns in coil 2}}$$

$$\text{acceleration} = \frac{\text{change of velocity}}{\text{time taken}}$$

$$\text{force} = \text{mass} \times \text{acceleration}$$

$$\text{change of potential energy} = \text{weight} \times \text{change in height}$$

$$\text{kinetic energy} = \frac{1}{2} \times \text{mass} \times (\text{speed})^2$$

$$\text{moment of a force} = \text{force} \times \text{perpendicular distance to pivot}$$

$$\text{sum of clockwise moments} = \text{sum of anticlockwise moments}$$

$$\text{wave speed} = \text{frequency} \times \text{wavelength}$$

$$\text{pressure} \times \text{volume} = \text{constant}$$